An Epistemic Review of
Human Rationality

The Delude

A PHILOSOPHICAL JOURNEY

Yoji K. Gondor

Author: Yoji K. Gondor
Content Assistant: Michelle Gondor
Editor: Brenda Strohbehn
Design: Chanjuan Liu-K

ISBN: 1481015370
ISBN 13:   9781481015370

Library of Congress Control Number: 2012922014
CreateSpace Independent Publishing Platform
North Charleston, South Carolina
To contact us please email to: admin@sintesipoint.org

ACKNOWLEDGMENTS

For her caring and support, I thank my daughter Michelle who was a significant encouragement in my effort to write, update, and publish this work.

I am grateful to Huimei and in special to my lovely wife Chanjuan who has always been considerate and sustained me without any hesitation.

I also thank my friends John Gavilla, Mircea Moga, and Dan Balan who have been along with me in my abyssal struggle of the last few years. Foster Glass was one of the first to learn about this writing, I thank him for providing positive feedback and encouragement. Much regard to my sisters Manuela, Cecilia, Felicia and their families. Thanks to my mother Marioara who always wished the best for me and all of us.

I appreciate the publisher for making this book's creation possible. Without their assistance, this writing would perhaps never have been printed.

In memory of Joska.

- *Delude: an individual who regards his own mental fascinations as reality, and is predisposed to strongly dedicate his or her entire life to a single idea which can be useful or destructive to his or her own life.*
- *What the deluded fool says typically is not right or even wrong; it is downright stupid.*
- *The concept of the delude forwards the inference that man is not guaranteed rationality but is merely capable of being rational.*
- *A generally accepted opinion is not, on that basis, guaranteed valid or a proof of its accuracy; equally, it is not proof of its falsity.*
- *Thought is not a physical object; it can only be understood by the actions generated by its exteriorization or projection.*
- *Some univocal statements can be, at times, equally true and false. For example we can state:* Today is Monday. *That can be true - if and only if - today is in fact Monday; this implies the cyclical real-time validation.*
- *Snobbism and a craving for superior social standing sometimes lead to bigotry and racism. This is achieved not by elevating yourself but by an attempt to denigrate others; that fits the deluded fool's route to fulfill* deludes *desired exclusive social status.*
- *The metaphysical description of God as 'that than which nothing greater can be conceived' is particularly puzzling to the fool's mind. Can God be the implied fancy of the infinity concept?*
- *It is self-evident that when we grasp that our understanding of our universe amounts to about nothing, then, in fact, we know something.*
- *We can create enemies by speaking the truth; however, they are better than the friends obtained by flattery.*

➤ *At times, facts are in front of us; the blind can not see them, the deaf can not hear them, and the deluded fool can not believe them.*

➤ *There is no profit in pleasure; only hard work can bring it along. And what do we do when we get the profit? Make use of it to get some more pleasure.*

➤ *An un-kept promise is like a rainy day: useless, cold, and depressing.*

Contents

Foreword

At times, the subject of philosophy is unjustly considered merely a pointless and entangled reasoning in a futile and conceptual web of abstractions. Some hoodwinks go as far as to consider philosophy dead or irrelevant.[1] In this writing, I seek to point out the inherent beauty of philosophical matters and achievements and the philosophy's timeless impact on the progress of the human condition. Of course, all this is also praise to the significant capability of the human mind and the immense intellectual achievements that are reflected in classic philosophical works. This book illustrates my delight in the study of philosophy and consists of thought concerning applied epistemic principles placed into modern context, along with practical consideration of logic, rationality, metaphysics, morality, and more. All this is considered in a manner related to casual human activities, and it is not purely a study inclined toward intellectual abstraction. The focus of this writing is a study of the familiar ways of developing erroneous comprehension or accumulating knowledge in an improper way that is presented against classical views of making sound judgments. I point out a number of universally valid laws/rules of thought and describe the established pathway to some sound natural or trained understanding. Furthermore, I reflect about some of the well-known defective views. I want to reveal to the reader opinions of logical implication along with the typical philosophical component of undeniable puzzling charm.

The passionate pursuit for sensible knowledge is constructive if, implicitly, it is accepted that the grasp of full and definite truth is beyond our natural or biological abilities. Without a coherent way to understanding, we become incapable of meeting contingencies of a mature life—a requirement that is essential for a civilized existence.

_____
1 *For an example see the appendix essay – The Philosophy is Dead*

In this writing I compare the generally agreed-upon view of reality and contrast it with the generally established defective view; a view that I assign to the intellectually deficient—the deluded individual.

Our mental concepts are the only basis that provides a context of the *reality* we can possibly comprehend. The coarseness in which we sense the physical world is not adequate in satisfying all the conditions necessary to the full and accurate comprehension of all elements or distant details of this majestic universe. The philosophical use of logical reasoning is essential for connecting isolated events or thoughts, and provides an appropriate assessment of multiple random empirical observations. We expect to see logically connected events, even when an event seems to belong to the mysticism that is impossible to sensibly validate—it raises many questions regarding not only the event itself, but also about our own capacity for sound logical comprehension.

Also mentioned in this writing are some instances of philosophical themes that have assisted me in improving my logical comprehension of diverse topics. By reading Aristotle I came to the realization that equality is of two distinct types: numerical and proportional. Furthermore, I realized what is required for a person to achieve *greatness*. A great person does great things and is not hitherto *great* when he or she is only capable of doing great things or only meditates on acting but never carries it out. The uncertainty related to the reality of recognized or anonymous greatness still needs to be clarified.

Hitherto, philosophy has had a fundamental influence on the development of human existence. Some philosophical concepts have a direct impact on society; some others have pure theoretical value and are a part of humanity's educational enchantment. The ancient moral philosophies of Confucius and the Daoism of Lao Tzu have eternally enhanced the moral structure of Chinese society. Philosophical views such as Buddhism and Yoga, which have been initiated in the Indian subcontinent, have encircled the world and continue to have a great influence on those who discover them. The philosophy that stemmed from Greece and the rest of Europe has deeply influenced the Western way of life: from Plato's *Republic* to perhaps communism—the greatest negative social experiment that was inspired by Karl Marx's work, *Das Capital*. A number of philosophical works can be qualified as speculative philosophy; nevertheless, they are of paramount intellectual importance. For example, Kant's brilliant discourse on *pure reaso*n definitely qualifies as *transcendental dogmatism,* and it shares the space with the spiritualism of some religions. This form of dogmatism is difficult to invalidate since the subject is presented in a neat, brilliant, and organized way; nevertheless, it possesses an obscure and insurmountable intricacy. Kant's work is simply speculative philosophy, however, the work is monumental in itself and evocative of the construction of a beautiful crystal cathedral—with the observation that the cathedral does not have an entry door and cannot be practically occupied for God's worship. The cathedral is only an object of timeless beauty, elegance, contemplation, and even of divine inspiration but it does not have a practical use.

Philosophy is, at times, preoccupied with the power of rhetoric for the sake of mental fascination, fancies, complications, and assumptions—not for the simple and direct description of the truth itself. Contemporary philosophy, it seems, has lost its straightforward way in the search for the truth. It wanders all corners of the thought in search for significance and sometimes infests the minds of others with baseless fabrications. Reading philosophy often feels like laboring in a gold mine where tons of rocks must be removed before we get to a beautiful gold nugget—a philosophical proposition of timeless beauty. However, with all the mentioned difficulties, it is fact that the subject of philosophy has progressed immensely in the last century. Attempting to minimize the contributions to comprehension by philosophers such as Ludwig Wittgenstein or Jacques Derrida is futile.

The foundation of this writing is varied and reflects my considerations on multiple philosophical topics. Some thoughts originated from my learning in school and from books; some, from the Internet. The main source for this book is my accumulation of notes with regard to philosophical subject. The book handles many ideas and reflections that sometimes do not seem connected to each other. It is like a journey in the world of philosophy that looks at old ideas in a new, modern context. It is now easy to look back and see discrepancies in the old philosophical work—now, when we have gained much scientific knowledge that has resolved many of the old-generation mysteries.

The intended user for this reading is an individual with a broad and varied interest in philosophical topics and concerned with the state of the human condition. Despite the richness of any language, occasionally the author finds it difficult, if not impossible, to identify an expression which closely fits a concept. I regret that at times I was not able to find the words to completely communicate what I was trying to articulate. As an author is seldom satisfied with his work and must at some point arrive to the end of his writing, I will consider it done only when the writing is abandoned. At this point, I believe that this writing will positively raise sufficient spiritual interest to be worth sharing with others.

The bibliography lists about 100 references, the majority of which are original sources that have inspired me and generated reflection on the subject that is presented in this writing. It provides the foundation of what I present here as the *agreed-upon reality.* The references provide a basis upon which an apparent and established classical way of getting to sound, erroneous, or even bizarre conclusions is based.

CHAPTER 1

The Way to Deluded Knowledge

The extent of knowledge a person accumulates is unequal among individuals with respect to both quality and quantity. As a result, individuals differ in both the details of their knowledge and in viable prospects to correct understanding—or comprehension—that is available to them. This clarifies the disjoined assessments among individuals regarding even the simplest and most routine events. Without a grasp of basic epistemic concepts, a person can pass through life restricted by the influence derived from the rigid mold of common sense, by the influence of commonly shared points of view, or with a strong and misguided passion. In this way it becomes deficient in the ability to deploy the essential constraint of obligatory, cautious, skeptical reason.

If the sense data received by the cognitive system is vague, then we have a wide array of solutions to be considered as potential paths to understanding. Accurately selecting the correct path, which ought to be chosen toward proper understanding, is difficult. Over time, I have observed a pattern of commonly accepted views of what we call reality—*the agreed-upon reality*[2]. Some of these views defy the typical way to comprehension; some have the outstanding capacity to see into the future clearer and further than most. Many of these individuals can attain the status of a celebrity and even the outstanding reputation of a *genius*.

On the other side of the range, a totally bizarre, but nevertheless familiar, view of a mentally mutilated and therefore dysfunctional individual resides. The strange being, which exists as opposite to the genius, is *the delude*.[3] The delude's main characteristic is that he or she holds a preponderance of delusional opinions that are assigned to common events or that spring from his or her intrinsic ability to frequently self delude. Large amount of falsehood, when regarded as truth, can induce severe damage to a person's intellect. The delude is an individual that is predisposed to accept as true incoherent opinions—some that his own cognitive system generates. We can perceive such an individual as a fool, a jerk, or even a normal person due to his supplementary personal traits of personality and character. At times, individuals are saying nothing while they appear to say something notable—silence can be, at times, improperly regarded as impressive eloquence. The quiet person can be attributed many qualities: thoughtfulness, temperance, moderation, patience, and respect. If that is rightfully so, it is another matter. If the delude is outspoken, then his or her mental chaos can be easily sensed, and he or she becomes what we call a fool—more *précis, a deluded fool.* The classical definition of a fool is equivocal; I do not envision him or her in this work as a jester—a member of a noble household who provided entertainment—but as a mentally deficient person. Even some mental conditions such as paranoia or schizophrenia possibly have *the delude* condition as its basis for forming, but that is not the scope or competence of this writing.

Even when a person is born possessing a healthy mental state, the familial and environmental assault during childhood with deluded opinions and behavior can be the basis for an individual to develop into a delude, an individual in a deluded mental state. In this writing, the

---

2 *The agreed-upon reality: an accepted view, a consensus of the state of an event or object.*
3 *Delude: (noun) is defined here as an individual that is predisposed to develop and hold illogical opinions of even the most elementary and basic events.*

label *fool*, or *imbecile*, is sometimes interchangeable with the under-lying primary conditions of the delude. A fool is predisposed to accept deluded opinions as true; however, he or she can have an overall good awareness of social norms and laws that he or she learned to comply with. A fool is not, because of his mental condition alone, a villain. In contrast, the delude typically develops overwhelming extreme views. These views can be held as more important than any social or legal considerations. Because of this, the delude is heavily inclined toward harmful acts and fueled by his deceptive extremism; he or she leans toward social rebellion that does not exclude criminal acts. The delude becomes frustrated with the imperfect world and is commonly devastated by the failure of his or hers absurd efforts to rectify things. I say that the delude is also a fool, however the fool does not have all the characteristics of what I define here to be the delude. The delude is more than a fool, he or she is an obsessive extremist fool.

The probable distribution of mental states will guarantee that an individual's intellectual qualities are randomly spread along the potential range—the genius and the delude exemplifying the opposite ends of the scale. Nevertheless, both are definitely and perpetually present. Hitherto, much attention and praise has been paid to the conception of the *genius* while the delude condition was somehow overlooked. Understanding the complex conditions that assist the becoming of a delude is meaningful: conditions that can trigger a person to have a painful, destructive, anti-social, and undesirable life. By joining the use of reason along with empirical observations, an attempt is made to describe a rational person's conscious actions. Also considered are some cognitive shortcomings supplemented with personal reflections regarding the defective development of the intellect. The delude is someone that habitually acts mindlessly and who can't handle an event contextually—not the wandering person that enters sporadically into the space of irrational action; a place that a common being conscientiously struggles to keep away from. The delude does not suffer from a physical brain deficiency; his short-comings reside in the area of accumulation of legitimate knowledge and an inadequate way to comprehension.

Adopting a skeptical perspective is not only beneficial but also required for properly evaluating logical concepts. There are times when an object exists in reality, although not within human experience. Without direct observation, an object is experienced by means of logic, which can often be misrepresented yet considered part of the state of affairs. Therefore, a sort of skeptical shield must be in place to protect the observer from possibly adopting illogical or unfounded positions. Only when logic overcomes the skeptical concepts—which sift out what is not proven factual—can the inexperienced events be considered valid by reason alone. Certainly, it is detrimental to accept as knowledge only what is personally experienced, we must allow the inclusion of indirect experience derived from the social context: both individual and group knowledge. For example, we accept that there exists, and have formed a mental conception of the continent of Africa, even if we never been there. The concept of the delude forwards the inference that man is not guaranteed rationality but is merely capable of being rational.

I point out from time to time some humorous situations. Humor itself is a significant and pleasant activity of the human mind, requiring creative imagination and also understanding. It is difficult not to locate a particular humorous pleasure in the observation of the foolishly mindless acts of the delude. The actions of a delude do not justify the inflexible judgments often exemplified; his or her actions ought to be regarded as random acts—acts disconnected from the common necessities of predictable behavior.

Various circumstances and contexts (understanding, social, religious) provide an opportunity to describe distinct situations that fit the mentality of the delude. While I was working on the manuscript, I wondered what the boundary is, or if a boundary even exists, between a conventional view of the world—*the agreed-upon reality*—and the delude's view of it. A delude is not a person who enters accidentally the illogical world of irrational behavior, the delude is a person who permanently resides in that unfortunate world. A genuine delude has no skeptical worries or awareness of his condition and will not entertain, even remotely, the belief that he could possibly be a delude. In fact, the delude is certain that he is not a delude; of course, his certainty is visibly erroneous. In this writing, the delude is simply an abstract container, allowing me to point out what I believe is a delusional way of understanding.

Psychology, it is said, deals with thinking as it is; logic with thinking as it should be.

—EDMUND HUSSERL

The foundation of our thinking, the basis of establishing knowledge, is formed early in life. What is the adult person's moral or social responsibility in the positive mental development of his or her children? Can we protect our young from forming a defective mental foundation which would not allow for sound thinking, a foundation that would produce endless troubles? The obligation to shield the immature from building a defective logical foundation indispensable for sound understanding later in life should be an important social task. Once the sound and proper mental foundation is formed, the young can easily acquire additional knowledge and have the proper starting point and mental capability for rejecting defective forms of belief. We should shield our children from learning inconsistent things, such as reading fiction, until their minds can distinguish between a true story and a synthetic one. If a defective foundation for thought is formed, the consequence is the likelihood of inducing unintended countless instances of irrational assessment. This has the potential to harm the individual and those near him or her. We ought to accumulate knowledge to satisfy the need of social inclusion, and we must guard that the accumulated knowledge is valid. Without valid knowledge, our lives come about as being lost in an isolated and unfamiliar place.

A person may imagine things that are false, but he can only understand things that are true; for if the things are false, the apprehension of them is not the understanding.

—ISAAC NEWTON

Politically, the condition of the delude generates the prospect that he or she will develop to become a goal for prejudiced manipulation, a target of a carefully crafted propaganda, and an easy target for the power of rhetoric—such as the excessive calls to nationalism or a similar craze. The seed that would make one person become a delude could be implanted into one's mind at an early age, and sophisticated plans could be used in schools to make the young disposed to empty nationalism and bigotry, with the expectation that the future citizen would become a *dummy*, well-disposed and easily convinced to support political faction plans. Acquiring the agreement of an educated citizen is not a trivial matter; getting the desired consent of a delude would be easy. The usefulness of the naïve and pre-biased deluded individual can have important political and social consequences, particularly in a democratic setting. The obtuse desire to keep the general population at a lower, malleable education level to cause the majority of the population to develop into straightforward fatalities for propaganda, is, at times, equally beneficial and frivolous. I have no knowledge that such an attempt has been put into action. Nevertheless, the idea of such an experience is not singular or unheard of.

CHAPTER 2

Understanding and the Delude

The primary evidence of our universe's existence consists of the structure of perceived mentally sensed objects that we possess along with the inferences we derive from them; that conforms to the acquired personal reality as it is symbolized in our current mental context. We are continually obliged to trust our senses; even in the cases of illusions, the senses themselves remain accurate. However, the perception rooted in the sense-data is not direct and absolute but diluted by various mental and biological factors involved.

No particular probability is universally probable: for what is improbable does happen, and therefore it is probable that improbable things will happen.

—ARISTOTLE, *RHETORIC*

I equate *knowledge* to be the totality of the mental objects that we experienced and hold—with our mental content.[4] The existence of mental impressions is commonly not feasible without our sensing of external objects, but we must account for such things as mental impressions generated by innate ideas.

Raw knowledge requires mental validation and, by inference, becomes an assumption that is subject to acceptance or doubt; subsequently, it becomes an opinion. The opinion is handled by our comprehension processes. It is evaluated and becomes a belief that subsequently and inductively becomes a new formed opinion. Plato's famous view that knowledge is "justified true belief" points to the proper validated knowledge. In this writing, the concept of knowledge includes the acquired sense-data impressions—raw knowledge—along with the accumulation of new and intricate mental objects that are a consequence of inference gained by inductive or deductive reasoned examination of empirical or rationalistic events—*a sintesi*[5] knowledge. Along with empirical and sensible knowledge, it includes both deductive and inductive inference, where sensible entails knowledge acquired through intuition or some form of intellectual perception. A new a sintesi judgment can also be partially rooted in an earlier-held belief. The raw knowledge is gained by sensual observation such as seeing and listening, by measurement, by reading, or by doing various tasks. The raw knowledge is merely an observation and therefore is logically neutral. The sintesi knowledge is inferentially established by our cognitive processes supported by empirical, innate or *a priori* elements; it is not always evidently identifiable as sound knowledge. A sintesi knowledge can emerge also as intuitive a priori knowledge stimulated by practical empirical observation. For example, the abstract geometric concept of a circle can be inspired by observing the full moon on a night sky.

The comprehension act itself also becomes a new a sintesi knowledge object we call belief. Therefore, a belief is a cognitively validated knowledge object. To achieve a sintesi knowledge, we can start by acknowledging a *basic truth* that is a form of knowledge:

---

4 *I am referring here to personal knowledge and not 'knowledge' stored in books or computers, for example.*

5 *A sintesi: knowledge based on observation or idea, coupled with an associated inferential or reasoned component.*

indisputable true, and used as a foundation basis for sound thinking. Basic truths do not require demonstration; they are obviously valid, their denial would lead to contradiction. One example of a basic truth: *Two halves equal one.* All proper understanding is resting on its logical beginning, the *basic truths*. It is also true that some knowledge cannot be empirically perceived; therefore, it must be inferred from associated effects. For example, we cannot directly see/sense electricity even when it's undeniably present; we merely detect its manifestation by flipping some switch.

Some truths—and even facts—cannot be established rationally. At times, facts are in front of us; the blind can not see them, the deaf can not hear them, and the fool can not believe them. The wall of skepticism and the imperfection of language need to be conquered before we can assert any knowledge as certain. The alternate way to obtain a sintesi knowledge is to start from a single proposition regarded as true and to authenticate it by other coherent propositions that are available to us and are supportive of its validity. Self-evident truth—at times accepted as intuitive—is the basis of rational understanding that can be the starting point for a sintesi-ing other complex structured truths. The basis of knowledge can be: abstract (*a priori*), empirical (*a posteriori*), or multipart empirical or innate knowledge supported by inferential or reasoned component (*a sintesi).* There are persuasive skeptical views with regard to the legitimacy of *a priori* knowledge's primary foundation; however, precise epistemic branches, such as mathematics, do base their core concepts on formal definitions. The *a posteriori* knowledge provides verifiable, objective forms of knowledge. However, our senses do provide us incomplete knowledge about the objects they examine, and that knowledge is complemented by our mental processes with additional elements generated by previously acquired knowledge. For example, we may see a dog with three legs. That will trigger an awareness event that points to previous knowledge which suggests that dogs have four legs, and a skeptical inspection of the event is deployed. For example, we also can see a car parked away from us, but we can't tell the brand of the car or if its engine is *running* or not. By getting closer to the car, we can acquire additional sense-data to grasp the model of the car and to observe if the engine is indeed *running*. My point is that we can acquire objective knowledge by our senses and that knowledge is verifiable but not complete. A sintesi knowledge is a contextually acquired knowledge coupled with the individual distinctiveness, and, because of that, it can be correctly called subjective knowledge. Sintesi knowledge is prone to generating of new ideas; some of them account for phenomena such as creativity. For example: it is likely that the combined knowledge about a portable CD player and the development of solid-state electronic devices has induced the creative a sintesi idea of a MP3 player and later of the famous iPod. Furthermore, the combining of two previously unrelated memory objects can become a new a sintesi object, even when there was no direct access to the empirical sensation about the object but only of the memory of it. The sensation about an object and its memory imprint is not the same thing.

I assert that any chain of reasoning cannot possibly have an absolute *a priori* initial basis; its cognitive foundation is inherent in our mental physical structures. I have observed that beyond the skeptical barrier individuals do not possess identical innate abilities to handle logistical tasks. A reasonable explanation would be that the brain persistently develops new logical structures that are genetically shared. Thinking itself synthesizes the mass of information available and orders it in a new way; in this sense, logically sound inference can be assigned to thinking and therefore, can account for undeniable progress. Thinking can, at times, reveal to us a new truth by connecting previously unconnected or concealed facts. It is again self-evident that the more one person knows, the more he understands that much more is unknown, and the task of discovering the entire truth becomes unattainable.

The granularity that we detect/sense in the physical reality is limited by our biological construction; however, we have developed many tools that assist us in collecting data regarding our universe. We gain knowledge of our universe by studying our planet and also by analyzing the rays of light, radiation, and particles that originate in some other areas of our universe that have reached our planet. We generalize our observations as universally valid and hesitantly assume that our small part of the universe characterizes the construction of the entire universe. Without doubt, we learn various things by leveraging the remarkable cognitive power of our minds. Furthermore, we also learn continuously of new things in similar ways by inductively extending the borders of our gained knowledge. By finding a plant leaf, a learned person can reconstruct the particular qualities of the tree that the leaf comes from, and logically can assemble much inference on the nature of the tree itself.

Some things are understood from careful study; other things are learned from practical experience. For example, there are distinct ways in which we can learn mathematics, a foreign language, or to swim. Theoretical study is sufficient for learning mathematics. For acquiring a new language, the theoretical study is supplemented by practical application; for swimming, the practical exercise is at the core of learning it. We also analyze former historical events; history provides us the knowledge needed to inductively acquire a logical and reasonable view and expectation of the future. The fool is not much interested in any of these ways and of the usual effort of learning; he bases his actions on endless sustenance from his natural intuitive ability. The construction of new judgments must be positioned on the knowledge foundation that already is believed valid by us; a defective foundation will cause us future unmanageable troubles. We must say that it is hard, if not impossible, to even suggest the possibility of comprehension by our mind of the full objective reality. We can even doubt its existence.

It is now generally agreed that it is no longer possible, due to the enormous amount of the collected scientific data and the complexity of the subject, for common humans to follow and understand the thought processes of modern theoretical scientific development. For example, only highly trained individuals can account for the ongoing development of the scientific discoveries that base their continuation on sophisticated mathematics, physics, or technological advances. More and more, attention to detail and skepticism is required not to abandon the rational/scientific path for the mysterious and synthetic way of unsound thinking.

Similar to intuition, a belief is not always guaranteed to be a form of effective perception; it can apply error in our mental processes and therefore, tamper with the validity of the overall perceptions. Psychology deals with such forms of thinking when the mental object is disconnected from any kind of logical valida-tion. False irrational principles generally spring from conflict with themselves or with sensory evidence. Is there a means to establish a valid and true connection between consciousness, the objective reality, or the absolute logical truth? We also must consent that it is easier to have multiple rational minds come to the valid/true assessment of an event than come to the same false result. At best, we must attempt to depend on *the agreed-upon reality,*[6] a view that is shared among a large number of reasonable individuals. It is not the best solution, but I can't even imagine one more suitable. This is what my inquiry tries to do: to point to some rational form of *the agreed-upon reality* and then to highlight the totally strange and disconnected view, a view easily proven illogical—the view I assign to the delude.

As an absolute concept, knowledge integrates the conscious and the unconscious mental content. For example, knowledge about swimming, riding a bicycle, or expressing emotion is learned, but the technique is not consciously identified before experiencing it. Knowledge presents itself as a puzzle; not all the newly acquired objects fit in, and it becomes established only when the entire puzzle is suitably completed. The total mental knowledge content will allow the rejection of illogical or hallucinatory objects, and in such situ-ations, we can say that our cognitive system is self-correcting and provides for a function of error/pattern detection.

Ignorance itself is defined not as the negation of knowledge but as a circumstance in which a conclusion is reached without the awareness of the absence of essential required component about the object or absence of the basis necessary for sound rational assess-ment. Furthermore, a person that has cognitive difficulties, even in properly evaluating basic knowledge that qualifies as *basic truth,* is named here a *prime delude.*

Delude (1): a person who holds an overwhelming amount of false beliefs in spite of evidence to the contrary. At times, a delude is incompetent to validate even a basic truth as a consequence of his inherited genetic construction.

---

6 *The agreed-upon reality: an accepted view, a consensus of the state of an event or object.*

Delude (2): a person that inherited faulty mental structures or accumulated improper knowledge that disposes him to be cognitively incapable to soundly validate simple information. Some essential characteristics of the delude are that he or she:

- Is an individual that holds false opinions against valid objections and is resistant to all reason.
- Is unable to correctly evaluate the validity of things that are fundamentally simple such as basic truths. Example: You have one apple and give one apple away; therefore, you have no apple left.
- Has a mental condition characterized by inadequately holding false beliefs and regarding them as valid.
- Is a person who involuntarily misleads himself or herself.

Delusion implies that the incoherent belief or impression is firmly held despite being contradicted by what is generally accepted as reality or that it was soundly refuted by a rational argument—this is typically a symptom of mental deficiency. A *prime delude* is not only a victim of an external act of delusion, but he or she self-deludes himself or herself by incorrectly assessing logically uncomplicated information. The delude stubbornly holds as legitimate illusionary views of reality that lead to a permanent general state of mental disorientation. From early in life, the delude accumulates erroneous beliefs that create difficulty in acquiring additional valid knowledge—an occurrence which undermines the mental foundation needed for logical comprehension. This state of mental development is the basis for future mental conditions such as: idiocy, stupidity, foolishness, or even obsessive conditions such as paranoia.

Commonly, the delude develops interest in some particular area and becomes obsessively and overwhelmingly preoccupied by that. For example, an individual will become interested in sports, and in particular, he or she becomes a football fan. The interest might become a source of delusion, and after some time, the individual considers football a vital part of his or her life that gets priority even over his or her career or family obligations. He or she will enthusiastically watch any games he or she can; all of his or her conversations will merge with talking about football. He or she will memorize all sort of details and statistics and rules of the game itself, and at some point, he or she will also use clothing similar to what players wear. Such exaggerations can also be related to: religions, health, physical fitness, political or environmental matters, and similar things. This is a way to extremism—in whatever form we can imagine it. Extremism, therefore, is a direct consequence of a highly deluded mind.

Before we can arrive at desired and proper knowledge, we must refine our capabilities for proper comprehension. This accurate and valid comprehension of basic events becomes a form of primary decision making. Without proper ways to correctly evaluate the simplest of events, we become unable to construct the basis for our future comprehension necessities, and we cannot gather valid knowledge indispensable to a rational life. At times we also must discard some acquired knowledge that has been identified as invalid, return to original thought, and start on a new logical path that expectantly will lead us to a new and valid understanding. For thousands of years humanity has accumulated knowledge, and any of us can grasp only a small quantity of it even though it is there, and available, for our specific use. I say that the trouble in acquiring valid knowledge is that we are, in a way, fighting against a faceless enemy that is allowing us to take appearance for reality. Many dangers undermine our path to sound understanding. Some of those dangers include: perception, belief, subjectivity, bias, emotions, intuition, guessing, illusion, rhetoric, faulty confidence, and even dishonesty. The danger of accumulating improper knowledge wrongly shapes the most important parts of our lives, including: family, social, employment, political, or religious life. The darkness of ignorance is what makes the reaching of understanding nearly impossible—with the comment that the absolute reality and perfect understanding reside only in the mysterious and abstract metaphysical space.

We must note that some univocal assertions can be, at times, equally true and false. For example we can state: *Today is Monday.* That can be true if, and only if, today is Monday indeed; and it implies a cyclical real-time validation. The statement *Today is Monday* can be determined objectively, independent of feelings, opinions, and prejudices; then again, it is not always valid. Our logical system is closely coupled with the concept of systematic time, without which it cannot properly operate. Time is essential for such tasks as ordering, and is indispensable for fundamental relations such as cause-and-effect. We must be cautious; in the absence of sound logical connection in reasoning we can assert that some effect might follow a cause. However, the logical connection is nonexistent; the cause is not the reason for the particular effect, and therefore, we presume appearance to be reality. Furthermore, the time concept provides a means of systematic sequencing the stream of actions that are chiefly packed with random events.

A generally accepted opinion is not, on that basis, guaranteed valid or a proof of its accuracy; equally, it is not proof of its falsity. Similarly, a beautiful and suitably constructed sentence that satisfies the stringent norms of grammar and eloquence does not guarantee, by that alone, its logical correctness. I seek to wonder in the space of human understanding primarily by the use of the theoretical rationalistic approach—by the use of the reasoned fact. Reason alone does not provide a path to direct knowledge; however, it provides the ability to properly grasp the facts. Reason only assists in sound comprehension.

Thought is not a physical object; it can only be understood by the actions generated by its exteriorization or projection. We cannot sense acts of thinking; we only observe a person's actions that provide inference of the thinking that leads to the initiation of such actions—that is, if we are not intentionally deceived. Therefore, an external observation of an action will be mapped to the act of thinking that leads to such an action. Sound thinking would imply that we hold our opinions if we do not grasp enough insight regarding the subject examined; any displayed projection about the subject would be a waste. If we project our opinion, by speech or action, about such an event, it will reveal our state of mind and expose some content of our thinking. In some cases, the action could attempt to divert our attention to the wrong or deceitful conclusion. Only the exteriorized projected intent of thinking can be directly detected.

We need to admit that from time to time hypotheses may possibly lead to logical absurdities or to vague transcendental opinions. Also, we must assert that moving from total skepticism to logical argument is not probable. It happens at times: the absurdity to which an argument leads us in assessing some fact is different from the absurdity some other argument leads to in reference to the same deed. However, when rationality, induced by logical thinking, is replaced with biased mental fancies or immanent impulses, then the infinity of wrong conclusions are the basis of choice for the mind. The way that leads to legitimate knowledge is provided by observation and logic. Personal opinions can be sensible and logical; however, as David Hume recognized, we must be careful that the empirical evidence of the senses does not contradict them.

To be validated and to exit the hypothetical realm, all knowledge and truth must be confirmed. It is self-evident that just because some event or quality is possible or even probable, that alone is not adequate proof of its existence.[7] There can be a substantial and subtle difference between what happens and what we expect to happen. Our wishes and desires cannot always be fulfilled; there is a willing of the possible, and sometimes also the willing of the impossible or even the willing of the absurd. It is useless to warn the thoughtless person that generalizations do not logically validate a particular event; he has mastered the way to arrive, with great confidence and pride, to erroneous conclusions. At times, we desire to have a particular exoteric conclusion of an argument or syllogism and then try to reconstruct the premises and the middle term by manufacturing so-called *facts;* that way we frequently arrive to some wanted artificial/biased conclusions. The delude is an expert at such compositions. The delude's ability to distort even the simplest requirement of logical thinking is definitely monumental.

It is inaccurate, yet I must say, that deluded fools are never someone we personally know. From time to time we observe someone who acts in an irresponsible manner—a pompous, rude, or vulgar person; an incompetent individual for whom reason and rationality is a source of inconvenience; a person who knows everything about all things and does not have the capability or willingness to listen and learn anything new; a person who opines about the unknown; a person confident in his arbitrary and unfounded judgment. In this case, you likely met a *deluded fool.*[8]

---

7 *A subject matter methodically researched and described by David Hume.*
8 *Deluded fool: an atypical or joyful person; he is content, confident of his phony wisdom, absurdly detached from any current or civilized perspective.*

I accept it as obvious that humans are deeply complex; it is next to impossible to completely understand much about their state of mind. Regardless of solidly founded opinions, I believe that we can act foolishly if we dare to advance a strong or inflexible opinion of anyone. We can always rightfully judge people's actions, but we should not attempt to judge the people themselves; it is not the same thing. A bad action is not an indication of a *bad*, incorrigible person; at the same time, a *good* action is not descriptive of an always *good* person. In time of crisis, one's character and abilities come to be openly known, abilities that others are not likely to foresee. If the delude also has natural mental capabilities which are below par, then sometimes he or she is also called an *imbecile*. I learned from a Japanese proverb a standard way to detect an imbecile: "When a finger points at the moon, the imbecile looks at the finger." The delude is a universal characteristic of the human condition—not specific to any ethnic group but belonging to the entire human species—and is bound together to others who are similar by means of their unfortunate mental state. The delude acts in a repulsive way: he or she ignores the world's perception of his or her character, and moral clashes with others are inevitable. It is safe to say that the delude is not an admired being, and he or she is certainly lonely in his or her unfortunate life.

We all realize that a little fire warms us; however it can grow and become hazardous. Ask the deluded fool to start a fire to warm us, and he or she will become an involuntary arsonist. Give the deluded fool a knife, and he or she will turn into a murderer. In the deluded fool's world, such exaggerations are customary. Talking to the delude can be a difficult task. When someone asks meaningless questions, as deludes commonly do, what is the merit if one answers them? At times, the delude becomes silent when he is incapable of a good answer, but he or she continues to listen. The silence is inwardness—not neutral but private, and possibly cowardly. Naturally, we know that only the dead are truly quiet and that the delude is simply hiding. However, if silence is indifference concerning a negative act, by that alone it becomes a spineless, pretend, and deplorable action that is an obstruction of realizing the fundamental requirements of an upright social life.

The delude typically takes things according to their first appearance, and needless to say, he or she arrives frequently at very odd and erroneous conclusions. This condition leads to a large accumulation of invalid knowledge and biased judgments. When prejudices have taken root in the delude's mind, it is a hopeless endeavor to attempt to seek the changing of his opinions. It is a natural aim of any individual to better himself or herself and to become the best person he or she can possibly be. On the other side of the spectrum is the delude's life. The individual can become *great* only accidentally and for a short period of time. We all possess distinct abilities to learn: some are innate, embedded in our genetic structure; others' abilities are facilitated by our acquired knowledge. For ordinary people, there is certain benefit in making a few mistakes early in life; that is not factual for the delude. The common person *learns* from his or her own mistakes, they provide a chance to avoid them in the future. The delude does not easily *learn*; the delude processes robotically any mistakes and turns them around, sadly, in a way that fits his or her character. The delude is a sad form of a human automaton. We can safely state that delude*s* are unable to learn from others; however, learning is an important undertaking that makes possible some understanding of the complicated world around us.

It is obvious that the capacity for logical thinking is not uniform among the members of a group. Arrival at the present human condition of our physical and mental capacities is a consequence of long-time biological evolution. I question if the emergence of the delude is avoidable; its appearance is factually a consequence of a mistaken and unfortunate condition that facilitates an individual in acquiring an unstable initial foundational knowledge. Once the illogical knowledge has taken roots, additional such data piles up in one's mind, making it nearly impossible to reset and start from the beginning in building a valid form of such foundational knowledge.

Numerous people—such as artists, scientists, original thinkers, or leaders—have attained timeless honor in an equitable way. In philosophy, the universal moral contributions of Socrates and Kong Zhongni[9] have endured the centuries and yet preserve inspiring

---

9 *Kong Zhongni: known in the Western world as Confucius.*

soundness and veneration. In mathematics and science, geniuses such as Pythagoras, Euclid, Isaac Newton, and Euler[10] have contributed in a resounding manner. For example, the mathematical truth presented by Euclid mathematics is eternal, and our modern mathematics adds to it new dimensions; it never attempts to doubt or repeal it. For travelling in space, we base our calculations on Isaac Newton's contribution to classical physics. Albert Einstein's vibrant and amazing theory of relativity has enchanted our senses for decades by its intellectual boldness and exquisite vision; however, the intricate task of proving or invalidating it is ongoing—a nearly impossible task that is typical with regard to any hypothetical advanced theory.

Some famous people have gained much prominence even though their ultimate merits are actually doubtful. Various military commanders have achieved vast power and fame by gaining military superiority over their opponents, by becoming impressive strategists and tacticians, by their readiness for battle, by using technological advances in generating weapons, and also by the use of barbaric-style cruelty. Historians place Julius Caesar, Alexander the Great, Sun Tzu, Hannibal, Attila the Hun, Genghis Khan, and Napoleon Bonaparte among the most successful army strategists and commanders. At times, war is judged not for the courage and heroism of the soldiers but, unfortunately, for the large count of victims or casualties. Many have made excessive use of their power that ultimately brought about destruction, including their own. Some have aspired to conquer the entire world, and the outcome was, time after time, a devastating failure. Only a delude (or fool) will set an aim so much outside of his or her objective possibilities such as conquering the world really seems to be. Not that long ago, Adolph Hitler followed his delusion to unite the world under his *General Government* by using the technical advances of his nation and the power of his army; now he is remembered mainly for his cruelty and the criminality of his war. Looking back in time, Hitler had no real chance of conquering the world—was he basically what I name here *a delude*?

We dedicate significant attention to the ones that surprise the common person by their totally ridiculous manners—conduct on

---

10 *Euler: Famous Swiss mathematician who is the author of "the most beautiful formula ever" ($e^{ip} + 1 = 0$).*

which this book attempts to shed some light. It is the abstract and lonely world of the foolish, of the thoughtless being, and of those in the similar mental condition that have gained our attention generally in a few writings and proverbs. This is the world of the delude that we see at times happy or cheerful only. To such a being, happiness is merely the attempt to satisfy all possible wishes; which is not even remotely possible. From here on, I will include some personal views and opinions, but please be aware that I might involuntarily cross the boundaries of the delude's world, and sadly, without being aware of it.

CHAPTER 3

The Mind of the Delude

The material world is real; the difficulty stands in our approach and capacity to determine it. I posit the opinion that the *spiritual* component emerged later, and that the material world first existed. The self-evident fact is that we, the human beings, are in essence mere collections of biologically clustered fundamental particles.[11] The physical matter was required to have been present before the mind; the matter has been the foundation for the creation which the biological structures of the life form. Later, the life form acquired what we call mind, and therefore, the mind is a consequence of the matter's quality and a proof of its existence.[12] I wonder about the singular moment when inert matter became life. The journey from the initial form of life to the spiritual human manifestation is a remarkable pathway.

---

11 *Stephen W. Hawking: "The fact that we human beings—who are ourselves mere collections of fundamental particles of nature...."*
12 *A materialistic view is that physical matter is required as the basis of our life form.*

The whole problem with the world is that fools and fanatics are always so certain of themselves, but wiser people so full of doubts.

—BERTRAND RUSSELL

Through time, life traveled from a senseless state to the development of sensory perception, memory storage, and the development of complex consciousness and cognitive states. After a life ends, the physical matter that fulfilled the life object returns to its inert physical state. Seen this way, death itself becomes only a transformation. Beside existing physical structures, the mind accumulates memory objects. The memory object is a physical impression applied to our brain structures; it can be acquired through sensory perception, emotions, innate thinking, or as the result of association of multiple memory objects; we call this knowledge. Various forms of knowledge are also gathered and stored in the memory of computer systems, and that is commonly called *data*.

The *data* itself is a basis of what we regard as raw knowledge. For example, we can see, in time, planes flying in the sky, which leads us to a new generalized object that is not generated by a particular plane but by our cognitive processing and generalization of the common properties of the multiple sensed planes. It is common knowledge that we can acquire by observation, and it would facilitate the availability of the object for cognitive processing when needed. It is reasonable to assume that knowledge is stored in memory clusters: for example, the memory cluster *cars* would include such varieties as Ford, Cadillac, etc.

One unanswered question regarding memorization is whether, by repetition, we generate a gradually stronger memory impression when sensing the same object or we generate multiple memory impressions of the object to improve our chance to identify it when needed. Beside the common episodic memory, procedural memory objects are stored in the unconscious part of memory and are triggered by events similar to those that generated them. For example, we created a memory object when learning to swim. The next time we swim, we are automatically able to duplicate from memory the previous successful swim-motion pattern.

The procedural memory is not an instinct; however, it acts similar and is so close that it does not make much difference. While awake, our memory continuously processes the visual-sensation objects. When coming home, for example, we are neutral when scanning our living surroundings. At times, we become aware of any visual or non-visual change which happened while we were absent. This scanning of our surroundings is done continuously at the subconscious level; this is a form of background cognitive processing associated with forms of mental processing such as intuition or instinct. That provides us with an involuntarily awareness of change in our surrounding by the means of the change detection of patterns. Further, it provides awareness events as a consequence of cognitive comparison of similar stored and new-memory objects. In our room, a large vase being removed when we were not there would be detected and turned into an awareness act, for example. Additionally, this undeniable event proves that the memory seems to order the memory objects with respect to what we call time. The cognitive processing can differentiate the presence or absence of an object compared to an earlier memory image. The memory objects are managed by the cognitive function, and decisions are made to dispose (forget) some selected objects. Some memory objects are determined to be unimportant. It is unusual that one person remembers what he had for breakfast last week. While this data is new, however, cognitive processing decided that it was unworthy of long-time storage and therefore discarded it quickly.

We can cautiously articulate that we can sense the visual color of an object only by detecting the light rays reflected by the object; obviously we are not capable of sensing the object itself. Diverse objects and events provide opportunity for sensual perception; however, they are not the sensation itself, as it is obviously widely understood.[13] It is commonly agreed that the human being has nothing to go on other than a collection of nerve stimuli that gather fancies generated by the world around. It is evident that in our sense experience, we only have access to representations generated by our nervous structures and not to the actual physical objects themselves.[14] For example, if we sense

---

13 Objects sensing can also be named the objective component of our realism.
14 Sense-only way to reality: a concept eloquently presented by John Stuart Mill: "In our sense experience we only have access to our mental representations, not to objects themselves."

23

a cup, the cup is not directly experienced by our intellect, but our optical nerves generate a self-alteration related to sensing the cup—a modification that is detected by our brain and that becomes temporarily part of our consciousness. But there is more than the sense experience in the human world. It is fact that the abstract ideas are not consequent from sense perceptions, but from specific cognitive processes, and therefore, from the innate power of the mind.

Regardless of how detailed we perceive an object, is it sufficiently adequate? For example, we glance at a rock, we see its shape and color and later we can determine its weight and tell about its chemical composition. However, we can not directly determine its atomic structures; what our senses detect is valid; nevertheless, not complete. We can supplement our understanding of the rock by inductively adding general properties that we believe are similar materials the particular rock contains. The external perception of an object is complemented by our mental processes with additional memory-stored data of related objects and also complemented by the inductive power of the mind applied to the particular object.

Simply, I say that our belief system is formed as a consequence of the cognitive validation of acquired knowledge, and later we accept the result as our personal reality. Proven knowledge is methodical, and true beliefs mutually support each other. If a false belief is held, the induced contradiction requires abandoning valid beliefs, and in this way, the new structure of beliefs becomes unstable. In many particular contexts, the epistemic requirements are uncommonly high, and it is difficult, if not impossible, for all our beliefs to count as valid knowledge. The cognitive validation that establishes a belief is usually a form of interpretation of multiple sense-data along with the contribution due to our cognitive processing. Data is validated in a hierarchical way; it can be regarded as: true, un-doubtfully true, desirable, maybe true, unlikely true, false, disgusting, and so on. The sensed data is later stored in the physical memory as a memory object and includes the impression of the object itself along with a component that encapsulates its properties.

For example, we look at the moon and store its physical impression, its name, shape, color and size along with the emotional component present. We associate this with the earlier-acquired properties of the moon stored due to processes such as learning or earlier observation. If we observe a nice flower, the sense object is a *flower* object with its particular properties. Also, let's say that the flower is red. The color red is also associated with an object, *color,* in our mind, and one of the color properties is *red*. However, even the color *red* is an object due to many variations of the color *red*. Therefore, it is not only that we store sense-data as complex memory objects, but also, these objects seem linked to other objects—creating a web of connections. It appears efficient that this pattern of storage also implies that our memory-object processing is in fact manifold and distributed. The life evolution processes have been responsible for developing such an effective system—not atypical if we take into account the overall biological complexity of human beings.

At times, the empirical evidence of an object is hidden by some transformation. As an example, sugar exists in solid form as crystals, but it is present in a cup of coffee and can be detected indirectly by us as *sweetness* only; this is a mode of circumstances the delude is not cognitively equipped to comprehend. The deluded fool believes that some extraordinary people can, in fact, walk on water, but he ignores the fact that water can also be found in solid form, as frozen ice, and that we all, in that case, can walk on it.

We also can not sense other people's pain; however, we can indirectly detect it from a person's acts of exteriorization of it and understand it as compared to our similar past pain events. The sensed empirical data is associated by the mental processes with other mental objects and then classified into areas of understanding—either factual, rational, moot knowledge or invalid/unsound knowledge. The *foundationalists* claim that the structure of our belief system inherits its validation from a number of undisputable guarantees (comparable to basic truths) that form its basis. In this context, our belief system, then, is seen as having the architecture of a house— with its foundation firmly supporting its structures. Also, the human anatomy will fit the foundationalists' paradigm—with the point that the entire system is constructed around a rigid structure. *Coherentists* take our belief system to be like a basket or a nest—with our beliefs mutually supporting each other as the inter-tangled branches form a basket wall to hold the object together rather than relying on their justification from a foundation block. Both these paradigms seem legitimate and fitting to particular situations; also, a grouping of them seems appropriate.

The delude's belief system includes malfunctioning cognitive structures that has an unstable basis with random and unproven characteristics. A delude does not posses any means to rationally validate newly acquired data, and he or she manages to assign meanings to it in a synthetic, objectionable way. It is the defective foundation of the delude's cognitive system that makes it next to impossible to untangle the mystery of his mental structures or to anticipate his rehabilitation. The deludes' minds goes much further, and their cognitive structures connect unconnected ideas; the result is that they arrive at unsound and annoying conclusions. Ignorance itself believably belongs to the cognitive power; inference or connection of multiple perceived, but unrelated, events is what gives the fool the possibility to dive deep into the dark area of the human condition. The perception, validated by the delude's defective mind, allows the fool to infer conclusions shameful for a rational being. The deluded fool enjoys sensuous consciousness; however, he or she processes it in such a strange way that surprises even the mighty devil.

In cases where the perception of an object is a pure hallucination generated by the delude's mind, the perceived object might not exist in what we call reality.[15] Now the real relation between perception and object is destroyed; only the empty perception lingers, triggering a mysterious chaotic mental state. This purely immanent mental process is separated from nature but inherent in the life of a delude. An object has properties that can be detected by our perception (human perception) but also properties that are detectable by our a priori, analytic mental processes and, furthermore, properties unknowable to us due to the absence of a base needed for our mental processes to be initiated.[16] At times, a delude becomes a very original and independent thinker; his or her way to achieve this status is by denying the common *agreed-upon reality.*

---

15 Reality: we refer here to the agreed-upon reality.
16 Simply implied here is the presence of previous experience with similar objects with properties that are inductively associated to the currently sensed.

We all memorize perceptions and associate them with other memory objects previously stored in memory; this is an automated process—not too much to do with the empirical reality. The delude assumes that he or she knows all the truth, and he or she is so delusional that he or she can not ever be wrong; hence his or her competing opinion cannot possibly count as valid—this requires it to be quickly discarded. Accepting especially external opinions would mean that the delude must discard some of his old and strongly held false opinions and acquired bias, and that would possibly undermine the entire foundation of his or her thinking. Once on the delude's way, it is very difficult, if not impossible, to return to a rational condition.[17] A delude's *cognitive plumbing* is defective, and the consequence is a continuous flood of unexplainable opinions or unconnected feelings. Only validated knowledge can let the holder be tranquil, and it provides shelter from the indecisive conflict of emotions.

An *instinct* is not simply a reflex but a robotic inherent disposition to a particular action triggered by some external stimuli. Necessarily, we must reject dogmatic views regarding instinct's nature and follow the strict path of scientific method in evaluating it. Instincts are present at birth, not learned, and are resident in the subject's unconscious memory. Instincts seem to be *hard-wired*[18] in the brain and commonly appear in every healthy member of the particular species. One such instinct belonging to the human species seems to be small babies crying when hungry or smiling when satisfied.

Intuition typically is connected to the meaning by the ability to sense or know automatically without the help of deductive reasoning. It implies the ability to acquire understanding of events without any inference and is consequently detached from logical characteristic of thinking. Intuition is a knowing—a sensing—that is beyond the conscious understanding and provides us with beliefs which we cannot logically validate. The intuition is not a form of genuine assessment; it can apply error in our mental processes with regard to particular facts and therefore tamper with the validity of the overall perceptions. The danger of empty intuition is that it provides an automated context for our senses, thinking, and actions. The genetic

---

17 *Once the deeply entrenched biased opinion is imprinted in one's character, it is difficult, if not impossible, to remove it.*

18 *Hard-wired: in this context, it means a physical component.*

transfer that is accountable for such properties as intuition is potentially responsible for the emergence of such mental conditions that the deluded fool is a victim of.

The *genotype*[19] of an individual is constructed from the merger of *genomes*[20] inherited from his or her parents. The parents' genomes inherit the genotype of their ancestors; therefore the individual's genome is an ancestral inheritance of genetic characteristics. The genotype of an individual also contains much of the physical characteristics of his or her ancestors—sometimes far back from the chain of temporal existence. The transfer of physical characteristics does not exclude structures of the brain such as logical structures and deep memory impressions that seems to be stored in the receivers' subconscious mind and that account for such properties as logical capabilities, instinct, and intuition. The inherited logical capabilities can be seen as a result of evolutionary elements that allow the individual to draw assistance from his or her ancestors' experience. Instinct assists the person or species to automatically adjust and deal with essential events, while intuition is generating acts of awareness based on inherited experience of the ancestors.

The intuition can be based on ancestral memory[21] of impression objects stored in the subconscious and activated in consciousness by select events. The intuition can be seen at times as irrational, can apply error in our mental processes concerning particular objects, and can therefore tamper with the validity of our finding. In such context, the intuition is an automated and primitive tool that generates immediate awareness regarding an event and becomes an effortless but arbitrary *decision-making* act. In the delude's world, the activation of instinctual events is triggered in a flashy way, which is not customary for its species. This is a mental malfunction, and observers interpret it as an abnormal behavioral condition. Also, when the delude becomes aware of an intuition event, then he or she again fails to process this information as typical and amplifies it again, and distorts the meaning of the event in a way particular to his or her defective mental structures. Does this inheritance of ancestral

---

19 *Genotype: an organism's genetic constitution.*
20 *Genome: the entire DNA content of an organism.*
21 *Ancestral memory: the memory that includes the memory objects of one's ancestors.*

genotype imply that once the delude's condition is constructed, it will be passed on genetically to the new generations of individuals, and that once a delude your descendants will also inherit a predisposition for foolishness?

Commonly, when a delude speaks, his message is expressed in a disorganized way, and nearly impossible to comprehend; this is a clear indication of his mental confusion. His words and sentences lose their meaning, and in his mental battle with communicating it reminds an educated man of the concept of chaos. Deludes are experts at developing erroneous acts of thinking in a loaded emotional layer. We know that rational judgments require uninterrupted logical connection from the initial premise to the final outcome of the conclusion at which they arrive. Deludes learn to live with the absence of a rational train of reasoning, and they can easily replace valid premises with some stemmed from their own synthetic/irrational mental processes. Most of the deludes are seen as *misologists*— people who do not enjoy logical argumentation. But the truth seems to be hidden elsewhere since habit is acquired; instinct is not.

The foolishness is a random and unavoidable human condition. The large amount of random events determines our fate and it is responsible for the emergence of such a condition. It is undeniable that randomness generates patterns describable in mathematical terms; therefore, the existence of the deluded condition is not only probable but likely—if not guaranteed. We ought not to underestimate the element of chance in the event stream of our lives; most are independent of our being and hopeless to foresee. Furthermore, our responses to the critical events are based on decisions that spring from random experiences that have modeled our understanding; this adds a new dimension to the complexity of our life experience. Bad luck and good fortune are both frequent and natural in our lives; both are random sequences of predictable events.

CHAPTER 4

The Delude's Way to Comprehension

Various hypotheses are, without a doubt, only baseless, imaginary and arbitrary fabrications of the mind. At times, we tend to hunt for formulas and observations that support our fancied generated assumptions and neglect or even discard valid detail that seems, at first, to contradict our incomplete understanding.

Where all is but a dream, reasoning and arguments are of no use, truth and knowledge - nothing.

—JOHN LOCKE

We ought to trust only what is completely known and is not possible to be doubted; furthermore, all our knowledge must conform to precise methods, such as pure mathematics, or it is based on accurate empirical observations. Human understanding is furthermore limited by the mind's imperfect power of comprehension, and by the natural inclination to prejudices or bias. Due to such difficulty, or even due to our inability to distinguish true from false, we are forced to occasionally regard the doubtful as certain. This prejudiced condition is accountable for damage or even destruction of the logical judgment, and it generates an intellect suitable for the deluded mind. In the social context, to be worthy of the name *deluded fool*, univocally a person is required to conclude that he has already collected adequate knowledge and life experiences and that he has a valid insight of the world surrounding him. He is inevitably self-centered, secure, confident, and enthusiastic to confront all or any contests of the amazing wonder we call life. There is no excuse that feels unreasonable or inappropriate for the delude; any excuse will furnish him additional needed confidence.

As time goes on, the delude gains greater and greater confidence, and this is the way he or she isolates and shields himself or herself from the doubtful and ever-inquiring individuals around. It's the deludes' mental structures that provide automatic cognitive paths to avoid any potential difficulty, and the response to any demanding situation is well prepared in advance. All the perceived agreeable intentions are instantly recognized, and the success reinforces a delude's self-confidence as the failure responses follow existing cognitive paths that lead to assigning responsibility and fault to anyone else. The frequent triumph in assigning fault to others provides a delude with additional phony and damning self-confidence. For some, a delude seems endlessly happy, and he might be ludicrously optimistic. This is a false appearance because the delude is disconnected from the time and/or place and/or events that happened around him. He frequently detects early a possible satisfactory outcome—the light at the end of the tunnel—and becomes joyful to that regard without considering the fact that it might not be the light at the end of the tunnel he senses, but the headlights of an approaching train.

The endless number of attributes of possible perceptions is also an obstacle on the path to certainty with regard to the acceptable view of an object. Furthermore, it is evident that various prejudices will place judgment outside the realm of rational space. Now comes the delude. This is not a suitable view for him since he cannot risk exposing his own concealed and secretive prejudice. How can a delude possibly consent to being prejudiced when conclusively he is incapable of grasping the concept of prejudice and its roots? Careful listening would help the reduction of the existing prejudiced effect. A delude is not competent, even with the best intention, to pay attention to a complex or a lengthy argument. Careful listening typically provides a good opportunity to defuse an opponent's argument; positive listening assists in gathering additional useful detail that facilitates an improved interpretation of a particular condition, it provides a path to better comprehension and guards against illogical prejudice. In fact, this is a disagreeable detail. A delude regards the suggestion for lengthy listening as empty words intended to disguise the simple truth that is early transparent to him and only intended to deceive him, and therefore, it becomes merely a waste of time. A delude automatically believes that he comprehends the root cause of things and that his own opinions of anything are definitely the necessarily valid ones. Indeed, from the beginning of the argument, a delude becomes skilled to hastily speculate about a conclusion; he is familiar with and very skilled at the art of *mind reading.*

A delude lives at the present time. For this individual, the past and the easy-to-anticipate future are easy to comprehend; in some limited way, he or she is comparable to a mystical prophet. In general, deludes have difficulty coping with changes that occur in time. If you tell one time-dependent truth to a delude, he may perhaps take that to be the absolute and eternal truth, and he cannot account for any temporal change. If the situation changes, the fool frequently assumes that there is some attempt to mislead him or her, because the changes that occurred in time are rejected. The initial statement that pleased the delude is the one he or she demands to be actual. Is a cherry tree blossom a valid reality? Yes, it is indeed, but only within the constraint of time—in springtime.

For instance the stone which by nature moves downward cannot be habituated to move upwards, not even if one tries to train it by throwing it up ten thousand times.

—ARISTOTLE, *ETHICA NICHOMACHEA*

The foundation of the delude's knowledge was built early in life; his or her character was formed in an unmistakably erroneous way that can be altered or improved slightly with education. A preparatory coaching of the mind is required for supporting rational inquiry and logical argument. The delude learns early in life to act on first impressions, to doubt other peoples' opinions or actions, and to base his or her judgment on initial reflections that easily lead him or her on the dark path of false opinions. When false opinions occur alongside strong emotional outbursts, they are guaranteed to generate strong memory impressions, to persist forever, and in such context, to prompt irreparable damage to the delude's capability of future sound judgment. The delude deploys reasoning that aims not at the truth but at the rhetorical triumph over an opponent or at unconditionally making his or her own position prevail. That provides the delude with a sense of pride, comfort, and superiority in his or her private world of *dystopia.*[22]

A deluded fool is incapable of perceiving or accepting what is true or what is false; only events that match his or her preconceived prejudice are validated by his or her defective cognitive function. One must discard the prejudice that the truth is required to be something easy to identify, well known, or easily proven to us. In thinking, we must gain knowledge of the endeavor for arriving at a sound conclusion, and we need to distinguish what is accurate or what is vague in the input data we receive. We must admit that truth is equated with certainty, and it is in divergence with irrational opinions. To gratify his or her enormous ego, the delude needs to ignore or discard any opinion that is not generated or easily validated by his or her cognitive resources.

~~~~~~

Ignorance — the root and the stem of every evil.

—PLATO

~~~~~~

Confident and secure, the delude does not suppose the need to learn anything new. This individual is hopeful that life will be

---

22 *Dystopia: a negative utopia: place where all is not well.*

improved by the prospect of chance alone, and he or she is avid and optimistic about his or her future reward of such endeavors that involve pure chance—such as gambling.

~~~~~~~~~~~~~~~~~~~~~~~~~~~~~~~~~~~~~~~

Highest are those who are born with innate knowledge. Next are those who get possession of knowledge by learning.

—CONFUCIUS

~~~~~~~~~~~~~~~~~~~~~~~~~~~~~~~~~~~~~~~

Changing an opinion when additional previously unknown or relevant detail is acquired is commonly and reasonably expected. The delude becomes frequently stubborn; he or she promptly rejects the soundness of any argument contrary with his or her preconceived point of view or after he or she has sealed his or her opinion. Not that the delude does not understand a changing element, but he or she dislikes to be seen as inconsistent or as doubtful.[23] A deluded fool considers his or her stubbornness a form of determination that provides him or her a great deal of tranquil confidence. The delude does not anchor his or her determination on rational thinking or on certainty but on his or her desire to be seen as unwavering. Gathering additional data can simplify decisions, but it also can make some decisions complex and difficult to reach. Simple opinions—based chiefly on perceptions alone, without the burden of logical explora- tion, or held without doubt—are those that fit well the mental condi- tion of the confident delude.

A delude is certain, secure, and without any doubt that people cannot possibly ever sense his or her intentions, for this would com- prise the use of an impossible endeavor to seize his or her cagily hid- den thoughts that are well disguised in his or her secretive mind. He or she feels a good deal of security and sanctuary in the concealment of his or her opinions or intentions and takes frequent actions under the gloomy curtain of deep secrecy while some others are not toler- ated to disturb or to scrutinize his or her privacy. Greatly shielded

---

23 *Not being consistent or not being always decisive is seen as a weakness for the fool, and he tries avoiding it.*

by secrecy, the deluded fool easily finds ways to take evil actions and, at the same time, decides to maintain an honest and positive self-image. He or she carries out unethical things, but he or she considers himself or herself to be safe from discovery due to his or her self-assurance that it is not ever probable, or even possible, for others to know the facts he or she hides so vigilantly. If challenged, he or she will illustrate a show of strong emotional indignation, and from now on, he or she will feel justified to do whatever wrong feasible to target the *unfair and negative person.* In such a situation, the fool does not value family ties or long personal relationships; the need for vengeance is so strong that it overrides any concept of moderation or civilized manner. The acts of a delude can become criminal; the gravity of the facts are no match compared with the desire or drive of a delude in satisfying his or her need for revenge. Revenge is a hidden concept that the deluded fool believes to be the root of suitable and rightful justice and a path to self-respect.

By doing the same thing over and over again, like diabolic machinery, a delude uncovers a pattern of himself or herself and his or her actions; if not for the inquisitive probabilistic representation, the life of the delude would be deeper concealed in the darkness of mystery. When a delude feels rejected by his or her peers, he or she becomes very angry and explodes with reckless and destructive acts of self-protection. Who can put up with the situation that an *intelligent and self-confident man* like him can ever be accused of things he doubtless did, when it is not even probable that these private acts can be established without doubt. When the result of his or her own actions harms the delude in an unambiguous and recurring way, sadly, his or her mental condition does not tolerate time to reflect or to calmly evaluate the valid cause of the inconvenience. His or her character foundation is so unstable, he or she bases his or her entire endeavor on the synthetic belief of his or her undeniable superiority, and he or she feels victimized, even oppressed, by the others near him or her.

Despite his or her inadequate mental condition, from time to time a deluded fool happens to have qualities or genetic traits that provide him or her some justifiable sense of pride and self-confidence. There is no boundary or measure that binds his or her pride and pleasure in his or her qualities; little does he or she understand that his or her negative character component does, in fact, nullify all his or her qualities. A delude's behavior is someway similar to a drunk. One can get drunk and not even know where in the world he or she is, and, in that case, the conflict with the social structure usually has a miserable outcome.

A crime is always negative; therefore, the punishment is the negation of the negative, and thus, even though unpleasant, it becomes a logical positive act. A human action commonly implies will and intention, but the choice for *no action* is also, factually, an *action*. Deludes do not do intentionally evil things; they do things that they perceive to be good or useful for them, and such things frequently become evil to others. It is said that if we discover that we made an error or did an evil act, it is best to apologize and repair the damage done by that action; if not, then the error becomes later some sort of a wrongdoing. Furthermore, the fool does not understand that to say something nasty and to revoke it is not the same as never having said it at all.

To have faults and not to correct them, this, indeed, is to have faults.

—CONFUCIUS

The deludes like to plan things. If the outcome of an action planned by a delude does not generate the desired result, then fault is assigned to something outside the delude's accountability. Later, the same action is planed again and again in spite of the previous failures. For a non-delude, the circumstance becomes increasingly clear that the action planning is the cause of the repeated failures. This situation creates a negative consistence in the delude's behavior; in this way, the fool's erroneous actions and outlook are damned to persist forever.

It is a general truth that: one does not know what one does not know. With additional discovery, either empirical or a logical element that is gained by reflection, more and more detail becomes relevant. That brings along additional physical or logical implications. It is always the case that at some point we understand that more understanding can be acquired and that it is indispensable to validate a conclusion. This is where the deluded fool's mind fails to attain a reasonable inference and sometimes travels along the metaphysical paths of occult, illusion, or even delusion.[24]

The delude might irrationally believe something that is true. Let's assume that he or she believed that heaven does not exist because he or she scans the sky during the night using a powerful telescope and he or she determines that the heaven cannot possibly be there, because he or she could not see it. One might accidentally believe what is true. For example, we have no good reason to believe that our friend is at home. However, we stop by his home to see him, and indeed, he is home—a coincidence.

As in the *Gettier* clock paradox problem, by observing a stopped clock we are inclined to believe it without skepticism. Nevertheless, the context in which the clock was observed induces us to believe what accidentally happens to be untrue. If the clock in the Gettier paradox would be stuck at an hour much different from the observed hour, then the observation context would induce doubt regarding of the accuracy of the clock. For example, if the clock was showing noon, and the observer had read the clock in the evening, immediately that would trigger an awareness event regarding the possible clock malfunction. We also have to agree that a stopped clock shows at least one time a day the correct time; it is just the coincidence of reading the clock at the time it is on that puzzles us. By sensing the clock itself, we cannot determine its functionality unless it has an *indicator hand* that shows the seconds—something that we are able to visually sense. In that case, we can become aware if the clock's internal mechanism is functioning without having an absolute guarantee of its accuracy. Furthermore, we cannot count the reading of the clock as absolute knowledge unless we strictly believe that the particular clock is always on time, and it cannot ever be stopped/defective—which is absurd. Furthermore, we can suppose that the clock involuntarily lied to us, and that is not unusual.

A genuine delude is never insincere, because he or she does not know what it is to be sincere; he or she frequently acts in *bad faith*,

---

24 *Delusion: any false opinion that a person persists in.*

and consequently, all hope for a good outcome is lost. Arguments end miserably if one side *clams up* when the individual disagrees with some of the opponent's statements; this is the *senseless outrage of silence.* As Hegel believed, the refusal to verbally defend a point has a barbaric root: the barbarians' language skills were not sufficiently developed to sustain a rational conversation.

Silence is often advisable but indifference is both criminal and wrong.

— CONFUCIUS

The classic saying: "Insist to stay in silence or openly admit your ignorance" is the fear which motivates a delude to be silent and makes him or her eager to avoid such a negative circumstance. Being a deluded fool that has not acquired any knowledge in his youth is like a crane that is standing still and looking for a fish in the middle of a pond filled with rainwater. Now imagine the confidence a delude gains, against the advice of many, by fishing in such a pool and being successful in catching a coy fish. The delude ignores the fact that the fish is not wild but got away from some neighborhood container during the storm. In these unusual circumstances, the fool's arrogance becomes agonizing.

Does a man of sense run after every silly tale of hobgoblins or fairies, and canvass particularly the evidence? I never knew anyone that examined and deliberated about nonsense that did not believe it before the end of his enquiries.

—DAVID HUME, *LETTERS*

Setting up a psychologically valid goal requires that the goal must be in the space of obtainable goals; this is a severe source of pain and misunderstanding in a delude's life. His goals are largely unreachable in a useful order or suitable time. The delude's goals commonly exceed the goals of his or her successful peers, and his or her attempts to overpass their successes rightly end in failures. This is due to the absence of required qualities or prerequisites.

A delude disagrees with everyone around him or her who has opinions he or she cannot grasp—even if this person happens to be his or her doctor or teacher. The delude's own cognitive power is always called on to validate any opinion or action. Even when it is naïve to do so, the deluded fool pays little attention to others' earned professional credibility. To absolutely trust others is not possible for a delude, even when their expertise and mastery of a specific subject is formerly acknowledged. The experiences and defective learning during the childhood years linger in the delude's mind; they become the source for the primary knowledge he relies on in evaluating matters as an adult. The knowledge gathered during the childhood years' remains eternally entrenched in our minds—in consciousness or at the unconscious level—and determines in an important way the manner in which the individual responds to life situations.

The human mind is capable of anticipation, and that is based on an extension of a thought to a new judgment, and therefore, this leads to a new *a sintesi* knowledge object.[25] It is the need for anticipation that has initiated the need to know and understand, and the need to go further and further into the unknown and that made the inductive, analytic, or synthetic discovery possible. This mind quality is essential in our universal endeavor of handling future events—of decision making. It is important and satisfying to arrive at proper decisions. That is attempted by means of personal determinations made and based on the cognitive processing of the totality of memory objects accumulated by the mind—by leveraging our acquired knowledge.

By agreeing that a sound anticipation is not always within our rational reach, we must acknowledge the presence of the unknown data—data not available to us at the time we are arriving at such a conclusion. We can decide, based on a probabilistic analysis, what the near future likely might be. The distant future could have its foundation based on the outcome of near future events; those near events are

---

25 *This judgment outlines the base of rational or irrational thinking.*

feasible to foresee, and the look at the distant future can be compared to walking on some stairs: every step is only understood as we move on, and it becomes the knowledge basis for the next step. In addition, when the near future is surprising to us, it, as well, alters the foreseen anticipation of any further potential events. The larger the pool of memory objects[26] we hold, or more details about such objects are actualized by the awareness needed to reach our decision, the greater the complexity is to cognitively process them, and therefore it is becoming difficult to arrive at an adequate sound decision. In fact, a decision inherently implies foreseeing the future, and the chance of this has been already earlier dismissed. Therefore, the decision making, even indispensable to us, is not more than a mindless adventure—an act almost impossible to be rationally validated. Only in the world of the deluded fool the decision making is simplified to a wish, a guess, or a selection of a choice; therefore, a simple task and thus eliminate the agonizing need of an endless search for a better decision.

Some decisions seem automated; such decisions are made without much mental effort or reflection. One of the automated decision-making processes is the so-called *common sense*. It handles usual events that were prior experienced or learned. As an example, common sense will dictate going to some known place on the shorter path if it also provides sufficient safety; common sense ignores the present particular need.

Common sense is the collection of prejudices acquired by age eighteen.

—ALBERT EINSTEIN

Common-sense based generalizations stand on facts collectively known and agreed upon and involve dialectical reasoning—reasoning that is common and *defeasible*,[27] and consequently fails

---

26 *Objects held as knowledge.*
27 *Defeasible: in this context, we assume that common sense assessment can be overturned by further events.*

the requirement of typical logical soundness. Common sense does not comprise the personal rational substratum of typical decision making; therefore, it does not possess the required objectivity for actual sound judgments. It is based on assumptions that we bring un-reflected to our experience—assumptions that presume things are as they first appear with the fallacious multiple avenues this condition can lead to. The concept of common sense has been called against and in resistance to numerous scientific advances and usually may reject calls to change or even to scientific progress. Common sense is sometimes said to be sound practical judgment; its denial commonly leads to outright contradictions. In this context, common sense is regarded as an obstacle to abstract or logical thinking; it has its basis in personal experiences and tradition, and it also has particular significance in the context of specificity of different cultures. Therefore, the common-sense judgment is suitable and can be used reasonably from time to time for handling simple, frequent repeating matters in an automated way; then, it can be regarded as sound, practical judgment.

Common sense is not fit to handle complex decision-making tasks; such misuse of the concept is fallacious. In a typical way, it would require a favorable reception of new development or progress; that alone is incompatible with the mind of the delude. He or she bases many of his or her decisions on that alone. Common sense is learned, and it does not apply to unknown situations; furthermore, it seems that it is necessary for satisfying the validation requirements of a particular condition as intuitive,[28] and therefore, it is linked in a physical way to intuition. The link between intuition and the common-sense object is always present. The counter-intuitive event never satisfies the requirement of common sense, and this is another logical link to intuition—an inverse one.

Because the automated common-sense decisions are pre-made or trivial and are not logically validated in the actual context, they can be called arbitrary. The common sense concept implies the requirement of logical reasoning as well as the necessity to collect sufficient amount of evidence prior to coming to a valid conclusion or

---

28 *Common sense: it complies with the intuitive view, and can't exist as counter-intuitive.*

judgment. At the same time, common sense rejects its own require-ment, and it becomes an automated, non-reflected, judgment which is not dependent on any cognitive or logical constraints.[29] Common sense and intuition alike are memory objects tightly coupled together, and they seem to share some attributes. Is intuition also a valid deci-sion-making tool; is common sense a subset of what we call intu-ition? Only with the condition that common sense in fact exists and is not inferred as a simple/primitive decision-making mechanism that provides us sometimes the ability to absolutely murder the truth.

The ability possessed by men without having been acquired by learning is intuitive ability.

—MENCIUS

One thing the deluded fool universally defies is the understand-ing of mathematical concepts. He or she wonders if these concepts are required in the social framework. Is the projection of pure mathematical truth necessary in the real world, in an empirical way? Or is it obligatory for the abstract mathematical truth to be projectable onto the physical facts? Let's give, for example, a simple addition: $2 + 2 = 4$. A delude is confident of his or her accuracy for resolving such an expression. But, if empirically, objects are applied to the terms, then the expression becomes equivocal. If we add two apples with two fishes, then the result of four is undefined. Four what? Wonders the perplexed delude.

To the mathematician, the concept of infinity is indispensable for describing indeterminate, boundless, or unknown quantities. Associated with the concept of infinite space or infinity itself, spe-cifically in mathematics, we define a starting point. For example, let's look at an axiom from which we can construct objects: later, by creating greater and greater units, they lead to the induced transcen-dental or synthetic properties of these units—units that continue to exist only as an extension of our capacity of abstraction. A number

---

29 *Common-sense: implies its necessity in the rational decision making, when at the same time, does not satisfy that requirement.*

sequence can be infinite; nevertheless, any particular number in the sequence is a well defined quantity. Furthermore, any segment can be divided in an infinite number of smaller segments.[30] However, any segment space can only hold a finite number of fixed size segments. Any object can be imagined larger and larger until we cross the border of transcendental assessment and the outside border becomes undefined or unknown. An object, as our universe, is expanding, and in this circumstance, it cannot possibly be infinite. For example: infinity + number = infinity is not a true equality; infinity + number = infinity + number is the true equality, and in this particular instance, infinity has ended up to be assumed infinite. Any object can be infinite in size, in our imagination, and that is a quality of our minds and not a property of any real object. Therefore, time can be perceived as a sequence of objects (seconds, minutes, etc), but time is always real, and it does not cross the boundaries of transcendental space—an action reserved only to our minds. Objects unknown to us in entirety, due to our limited power of perception, should remain defined as unknown and not as part of our speculative/a priori assessment. As we comprehend now, infinity is an atypical concept and does not follow the established mathematical properties of numbers. For example: infinite/infinite; infinite*0; 1**infinite; 0**infinite; infinite**0; infinite-infinite, are examples of indeterminate expressions.

The limit of any quantity divided by zero leads to infinity. As an example, five divided by zero leads to infinity. If I have five dollars, and I don't share it, then will I have it forever? Is that what it really means? Yes, the delude contemplates the indeterminate form of the infinity, but he or she hopes that someday the truth about all this will become clear to him or her. This is based on the hope that the only thing he or she has to do is to be patient…very patient. When we learn counting, we make the tacit assumption that every integer has a successor, and that clearly leads us again to the concept of unbounded quantity, the infinite. The fundamental geometric object, the straight line, is based on the assumption that we can extend a line indefinitely in both directions. Can we even have mathematics without the concept of infinity? In mathematics, we have the necessary numbers: zero, one, infinite. Zero is the origin; the measure

---

30 Based on Georg Cantor's set theory

between the zero and one is the scale of the mathematical object, and infinite is the limit of the sequence. The subject is even additionally complex; we have to note that infinitum contains, besides integers and rational numbers, irrational numbers too. Mathematics requires the concept of infinity; it is used as a number but is not a part of any number set. Some real number cases—such as $\varpi/2 = 2*2*4*4*6*6/1*3*3*5*5*7*7*8...$—prove that real numbers can sometimes be represented by an infinite series. This property was distinctively recognized by the mathematician John Wallis (1616–1703)

In our world ruled by random events, can all of this ever lead to any continuous/infinite series, or can only the concept of time possibly provide such an abstract framework? Infinite sets violate one of our deepest-rooted experiences: *that the whole is greater than the part.* There are as many points along an infinite line as there are on a finite segment of it. We also can assert that if the entire universe were to be filled only with abstract mathematical points, the universe would still be empty, as the mathematical point is merely a concept. We learned about the peculiar properties of infinite sets.[31] Is our universe infinite, or does it have an outside boundary beyond which it does not exist? The possibility of the universe's being finite or infinite seems to defy our natural senses, for it isn't clear that we can go forever in any direction without reaching the edge. Is our universe bounded or unbounded?

Common sense is a very inadequate tool for dealing with the concept of infinity. As noted by the German scholar Nicolaus de Cusa (1401–1464), the infinite can have neither a center nor a circumference; rather, any point could be viewed as a center: just as to any observer at sea, the horizon seems to be equally distant in all directions, regardless of the observer's position. Our understanding of the universe does not comply with this description; therefore, we must accept that the universe is finite.

a) The universe started with the *big bang* of some singularity from a point that can be considered the center of the universe; this defies the condition that the infinite has no center.

---

31 *Georg Ferdinand Ludwig Philipp Cantor (1845 – 1918) was a German mathematician; he is best known as the inventor of set theory.*

b) The universe is said to be expanding (proven by Hubble[32] discoveries); expansion implies a moving boundary, which is inconsistent with the definition of the infinite.
c) The size of the universe is estimated by astrophysicists to be 10*12 light years; therefore, it is significant but finite.

With the agreement that our universe is finite, we can reasonably ask the question: Is there only one object that we now call the universe? I am not aware of evidence that there is either one or many such galactic objects as the one we belong to; also, there are no logical restrictions that it must be unique. We can reasonably imagine that in space exist many objects outside ours that belong to the universe. Also, we can speculate that our galactic object can potentially be a part of some other grandiose universe object. This enters the space of metaphysical inquiries that are difficult to estimate—if not impossible. Metaphysics must be proven certain, and not only be seen as probable, to be logically validated. That only fits the devil's colossal powers. Many times we base our reasoning of abstract propositions. However, abstraction itself is beyond the realm of actual time or actual physical space, and uncertainty will emerge when we apply abstract concepts to real-world elements. Furthermore, scientific knowledge ought not to be based on unfounded assumptions even if later the assumptions are proven valid.

A delude commonly struggles in handling concepts such as formal logic or mathematics. Arithmetic sets up laws for the relationships and combinations of numbers; however, colligating and counting the numbers are cognitive activities—tasks not suitable for the mind of a delude. A delude's mathematical knowledge can sometimes be limited only to counting—especially counting money.

---

32 *Edwin Powell Hubble was an American astronomer who profoundly changed our understanding of the universe by demonstrating the existence of galaxies other than our own.*

CHAPTER 5

The Public Life of the Delude

Disallowing in itself forbids a particular action, and as a consequence, it commonly induces a passionate desire for disobedience—that is self-determination. An anticipated risk of a reprimand is the penalty one has to accept as a price for satisfying the need for such independence. Tell a person that he or she is forbidden to do no matter what, and he or she might feel a burning desire to do just that. You have infringed on his or her freedoms; kids are notorious for acting this way. That is a basis for the thought that having too many rules, laws, or demands generates a state of revolt. A foolish person genuinely considers that all the laws and regulations are enacted to protect and to sustain only worthy people—especially those as distinguished as he or she is. This individual supposes that he or she belongs to an honored group of people similar to himself or herself and that most other people do not deserve such sympathetic attention. The delude can become truthful and honest when it fits his short-term, distinct personal necessity. He is a philanthropist, racist, bigot, or environmentalist, and is shameless about whatever gratifies his present-day need.

In the part of this universe that we know there is great injustice, and often the good suffer, and often the wicked prosper, and one hardly knows which of those is the more annoying.

—BERTRAND RUSSELL

Why do we demand equal and free rights for everyone? In fact, if everyone were to be seen as equal, it would not do justice to the delude's world. To be equal implies the need to be free, and freedom is an equivocal concept. The deluded fool imagines that he or she is above the basic requirements of the common law and is above the basic requirements of typical individuals; the delude is like a monument that ought to be admired but not troubled with too many rules. He or she makes promises that he or she does not intend to keep. This person is not aware that an un-kept promise is like a rainy day: useless, cold, and depressing! There are myths of racial superiority, religious superiority, or intellectual superiority, and these are truly joyful myths to the deluded fools; they perceive to belong to all these groups.

The delude is an individual who will strongly dedicate his or her entire life to a single idea which can be useful or destructive to his or her own life. For example, the reasonable population will not abuse the privilege to own a gun, but the criminals will; that is the proven way. One can perish by swimming in the lake, can be burned by fire, can be killed by driving a car, or by flying in an airplane. (In fact, flying in a plane is pleasant; the possible crashing and burning is the setback.) We do not ban the deep water, the fire, or the fast ways of transportation because of their danger to our lives, but we tend to desire to ban guns that are merely inert objects intended to provide self-protection or a sense of security. No doubt, guns are only designed to injure their target. While water, for example, is indispensable for sustaining our natural life, guns are not, and there lies the fundamental difference and divide. We can have guns or not; it makes little real difference for our species survival. We also can say that guns can be dangerous if handled by deluded fools; however, that is simply an opinion. It is obvious that we should outright disallow crime and criminals, and then the need for guns would be only justified by the necessity related to their use for entertainment.

It is our responsibilities, not ourselves that we should take seriously.

—PETER USTINOV

When a delude is in the position of power, much harm will be done to anyone in his path. People will suffer; they will be wrongly incarcerated if a delude's effort succeeds. The deluded condition and behavior are not yet formally acknowledged. We might necessitate acquiring an official certification for anyone we call here a deluded fool, and specific legal provisions need to be enacted to protect the general population from such a miserable and dishonorable condition. Until we are capable of achieving that, we'll not find the collective harmony of mind and the tranquility we, as a society, seek.

Deluded fools deeply believe that the only path to achieving peace is to violently destroy whoever is seen as an enemy. They are unable to grasp the difference between some group of victimized people and the government that oppresses them. Peace by violence is an absurd, but not an unheard of, concept. Commonly, wars are waged against armies and soldiers and not against civilians or their property. But deluded fools will not be stopped by wanting to kill anyone—even when only slightly associated with the perceived enemy. An appeal to patriotism or nationalism is not a confirmation of some *wrongdoing* or a guilty sentence of our rivals; although, the deludes are certain to accept this as proper. The deludes' feelings of certain superiority do give them much confidence in their powers, and in fact, they seem not to fear anyone in their arrogant actions. We must fear those who fear nothing, for they do not follow the natural desire for self-preservation. In war, the deluded fool is either the shameless coward or a fearless hero. His or her disregard, or the absence of understanding, of the field dangers of war makes him or her bold in taking reckless action that others consider too risky.

We all shall agree that the safeguard of a person's property is a principal obligation of any progressive state. Deludes are hypersensitive concerning their material possessions; it allows them to illustrate authority and noticeable significance. The unequal economical development of countries, along with cultural differences, has created places in the worlds far away where the population has preserved a simpler way of life; the people living there are sometimes perceived as *barbarians*. That reassures him or her of the privileged place he or she enjoys as belonging and being a part of a particularly advanced society—if that happens to be the case. We all learn that conflict involving society and the individual is not a meaningless theoretical issue but a matter of negative and tragic personal experiences. Nothing can be further from the truth than the evaluation of facts that are based solely on political interpretation, but the deluded fool will not agree with an opinion that he labeled ridiculous. The deluded fool's mind grasps these circumstances in a way consistent to his or her character; this is neither the right way nor even a wrong way; this is the fool's way.

Deludes can demand that certain services be made available to them by the city—at times without realizing what is possible and what is not. For example, the delude is not able to grasp that the city is not there to pick up the trash after you, but it is there to provide the bucket so you can place your trash in it.

As it ought to be, our government is attending the obligatory requirements of our money-oriented society. A government falls short in its duties if it fails to make valuable the capable, worthy citizens. The essential need of the ordinary citizen and the corporate structure are occasionally not supportive of each other; at times, they are contrary. However, the government is obliged to act in the best interest of the country in such a way that its measures will meet the need of the common person and also facilitate a sound environment for corporate operation. At times, the corporate need is different from the need of the social structures, and a brutal conflict can arise. The government must choose the side it will endorse.

A political dialogue that now and then can be rightfully called a clash will often occur. In such a circumstance, the faction that poses a large amount of resources (such as money) will use its assets and operate to influence (or buy) the naïve voters as a means of swaying the government's actions.

> *For a privileged minority, Western democracy provides the leisure, the facilities, and the training to seek the truth lying hidden behind the veil of distortion and misrepresentation, ideology, and class interest through which the events of current history are presented to us.*
>
> —EDWARD S. HERMAN AND NOAM CHOMSKY, *MANUFACTURING CON$ENT.*

It appears that our mind accepts, as a form of knowledge validation, the presence of multiple interrelated sensations regarding a singular event without additional burden of proof. The accumulation of sizeable amounts of interrelated sensed knowledge (not necessarily true or even rational) is capable of producing a continuous state of overwhelming awareness of an event and inducing an obsessive concern with regard to the particular situation. The awareness is strongly validated this way, and, at times, irrationally held as absolute and is accompanied by a strong emotional element. This is without doubt a strange property of the mind, which is widely exploited for a number of reasons—mainly in advertising or for political motivation.

Propaganda is a method in which the same statement is repeatedly publicized until the listener's cognitive function is overwhelmed and accepts the event as truthful—even when a cautious consideration of the message would prove it to be untrue, partially true, or a direct lie. This devastating and obsessive form of mental awareness can become overwhelming for a person, and in this way, it can cause severe problems. Propaganda's success in manipulating cognition and shape perceptions makes it a dangerous tool that should be prohibited. The matter becomes overwhelmingly significant for the particular person, and the continuous awareness of the event brings about an obsessive state of mind. Regardless of whether such a fixation is political, religious, nutritional, environmental, or about health concerns—it can become a form of extreme preoccupation. For example, the obsessive concern and unremitting awareness about environmental issues can be fairly compared to a deep and overwhelming religious experience.

The common victim of well-crafted propaganda is the person who does not possess enough capacity for proper comprehension and is vulnerable to calls to patriotism or nationalism, half-truths, or slogans and who is sympathetic to points he or she beforehand prefer. The wise commonly make their own decisions; the ignorant are not capable of that and are generally compelled to follow a suggested opinion. I wonder if it is possible that certain groups would find it irresistible that many citizens remain in a mental state that allows this sort of mental manipulation. In such an absurd state of affairs, groups would manipulate the schools to limit the amount of logical knowledge a student is exposed to, and it would impose that the student become sensitive and respond strongly (and proudly) to calls to patriotism, for example. In this situation, the delusional voter might have the characteristic that will allow being effortlessly prone to cast his vote as preferred by a controlling block of society.

You cannot easily influence the best and the brightest about false political points by using political propaganda; that is an easy task only when the targeted are the foolish people. Our democracy is based on numerical and not proportional equality, which would favor the inclination for having more people in the *dumbest* category—the ones more predictable to successfully control. It is beneficial for certain specialized groups that the number of easily controllable people is rather large, and there is a wish that the common citizens complete their basic education in such a matter that they become easy targets of such acts of propaganda. This sort of coercion is not direct but developed in subtle ways: such as the use of *educational lobbying* ads just before an election. Those are the ads which are not defined to be political but encourage the listener to take some preplanned or indirect political action. One good example is the conflict between the corporate necessity during the industrial *globalization* and the conflicting social need of a post-industrial society. The corporations themselves are neither sensitive nor do they have responsibility for the social well-being; nevertheless, their powerful influence on the body of government creates the conditions for the increased social misery, and that because social responsibility is not a useful component of the corporate progress. A delude easily falls for the carefully staged corporate propaganda and becomes a strong supporter of whatever the corporations wish for, even when it happens to harm self benefit in the process.

Another worthy example would be the current *global warming* condition where a few corporations, that are prone to lose revenue due to increased pollution controls, are convincing people of their point by using nonsensical means of persuasion. Sometimes, even phony scientific knowledge is promoted based on political or business interests. This sort of rhetoric is commonly directed at the deluded fools. We should possibly disallow the deluded fool to vote, but that would require us to properly identify the development of the person's regretful mental state—which is not reasonable to expect.

Being the citizen of the state, no matter how little influence his or her voice may have in public affairs, it is required of him or her to do his or her basic duty of providing his or her opinion and preference and to cast an election vote. At this time, our democracy implies inclusion of our species only, the humans, and ought to guarantee the inclusion of all members of a society. Regrettably, some omission exists for such conditions as incarceration or mental health. It does not seem significant that a number of non-convicted criminals happen to be free, and therefore, they are capable to cast a vote. Allowing the incarcerated to vote also would facilitate their inclusion in society, and it would assist in their successful and desired reintegration. If those incarcerated were subjected to mindless acts of oppression and joined the anti-social life from the need for self-preservation, then their miserable condition deserves a voice. At times, oppression is the root of social criminality, and it is the oppression that has to be prohibited for the situation to return to normal.

The democracy is based on counting the electoral votes, and the side with the larger quantity of counted numbers wins the particular contest. The individual vote has the same weight if either is carried out by a mother or by a whore—with the observation that a whore also can become pregnant and therefore become a mother. Democracy must be required to guarantee the absolute inclusion of every member of society; no exception is sensible. As I mentioned earlier, the deluded mental condition can induce a person to vote against his or her own personal interest or as influenced by others. Allowing the deluded fools to vote does harm to a democracy. At the same time, as my belief already stated is that everyone must be included; this seems to be a paradox that cannot be resolved. The danger would be in the intentional *creation* of large numbers of deluded and foolish minds by certain social segments, thus it would distort our true democratic balance and principles.

We hang the petty thieves and appoint the great ones to public office.

— AESOP

At times, the delude wishes that he were a decent and good person, and a respectable member of society. Yes indeed, a delude has no proper or sophisticated awareness of such a concept and destroys himself in the act. The extreme acts of goodness the deluded fool can think of are a shrine of carelessness, a misunderstanding of what good is, and a confusion of what a just action requires. In this way, the fool becomes unjust; and the unjust is malicious to everyone: just or unjust alike. A delude is ignorant of human nature; it is possible that a just man can do well to bad people and harm the good people. That is not justice, but in the fools' world, it is the norm. A just person is generally honored by society and is commonly expected to be so. The unjust is penalized by society when the opportunity emerges. Therefore, the life of the unjust person is unpredictable; in some way it can even become dangerous, and he frequently has to adapt to circumstantial changes and generate a sense of insecurity that is very unpleasant to the fool. Doing just or unjust things are also conditional upon any consequence and on any foreseen reprimand. Let's envision that just and unjust people will both wear certain magic rings that can turn them invisible. What can we guess the actions of the just person or unjust person could be? Could it be that the just man or woman can become unjust when the fear of the consequences of being unjust fade away? It is commonly agreed that the powerful are more likely to be unjust because negative consequences are not expected.

A man who wounds and harms us by intention becomes our enemy over that account. This is not the case regarding the deluded fool; if he or she harms us, many times it is unplanned or unintentional; nevertheless, he or she might regard himself or herself as a friend to everyone. Safely, we can say that we should be *good* with people of right action, and *just* with people of evil actions; therefore, the actions, but not the people, should be what we judge. Bad people, if they even exist, can occasionally do good things. Injustice against one single person can be seen as small or insignificant unless the victim happens to be you. Along these same lines, a delude that is also ignorant of the human nature can have bad people he respects as friends and consider many good people as enemies.

As an environmentalist, a delude is not equipped with the cognitive capability that would make it possible for him to grasp a situation's multiple perspectives. The deluded fool cannot detect the *disjointed points of reference*[33] of a particular situation. For example, if a delude acquires awareness and concern about the forest, he or she will not be capable of finding an understanding that will allow for the trees, animals, and humans to coexist in such a space. Sometimes a delude will devote his or her life to a cause such as the protection of the environment when failures in his or her social life develop into an intolerable inconvenience. The delude will become an environmental extremist; not too much else can be expected. A disconnect between his or her own negative impact on the environment and the environmental cause he or she cares much about is generally the rule.[34]

Occasionally, environmental evils are ignored when some destructive action is also able to produce profit so great that it influences bodies of the government, and the protection of the natural place or the environmental issues are disregarded. In the deluded fool's world, both the environment and the need for our natural resources cannot be mentioned in one single sentence. His or her mind would not allow any potential rational and civilized dialogue

---

33 *See the Disjoint Points of Reference essay at the end of the book for additional detail.*

34 *For example, the fool loves an untouched/pristine forest; nevertheless, he'll drive there with his oversized monster polluting truck.*

regarding his cause. He or she cannot tolerate, and rejects, any calls to restraint or conciliation. He or she will join news or environmental organizations that will pressure the government into doing things they should not do or even attempt to pressure government to do things that they cannot possibly do. He or she considers only his inflexible view to be important. No rational dialogue of this matter is even feasible; the deluded fool has made up his mind, and it is not mutable.

Our constant discontent and selfishness are, for the most part, rooted in the impulse of self-preservation and the doubt of our real social status. Snobbism and a craving for superior social standing sometimes lead to bigotry and racism. This is achieved not by elevating yourself but by an attempt to denigrate others; that fits the deluded fool's route to fulfill his or her desired exclusive social status. Some deludes are frenzied by racism and bigotry and lack the realization that racism and bigotry are factually irrational. One has the right to dissent, a right to side with anyone, and even a right to be an idiot. However, he or she has no right to lie and to hide bigotry as a political view. Sometimes racists know full well what they stand for, they but will simply deny that some attitudes and policies are racist. That such a position is indeed merely an apparent form of empathy is rather clearly expressed by one's denial of factual discrimination and racism as a major problem of any mixed society.

Only a few realize that the weaker citizen's civil rights must, as well, be vigorously protected. The shameful group of the deluded fools becomes the victim of false opinions and victimized by the careless use of the power of eloquence. In a democracy, we assume that people are well informed and have a decent opinion of their need. The delude's confusion is also present with regard to the choice of his or her vote. Should he or she cast the vote for his or her own private benefit or vote for the *common good* as sometimes he or she is misled to do by rough politicians? Even when a delude believes in the concept of democracy, seldom does he or she also believe in equality or even civil rights. Without liberty, *free choice* does not exist; in such circumstances, it is not possible to achieve a genuine democracy.

Absence of liberty is responsible for the emergence of various forms of oppression. Liberty, and therefore, the protection of civil rights, is essential for a democratic society; even the unappreciative deludes must be included. It also would be appropriate and unselfish if we would allow the inclusion in the democratic issues of all other species: for example, the birds or fish. We can also envision an extended democracy in which all species of animals, plants, forests, rivers, states, planets, and even stars systems representation can be included. For far too long, the human species has regarded itself as self-important in an absolute way, and the relationship to other species is as a downright form of despotism.

~~~~~~

Does a man of sense run after every silly tale of hobgoblins or fairies, and canvass particularly the evidence? I never knew anyone, which examined and deliberated about nonsense that did not believe it before the end of his enquiries.

—DAVID HUME

~~~~~~

The delude is commonly fearful of changes, and for that reason alone, he disguises his worries and rejects political changes that are seen by most as progressive. We know that sometimes the scientific view is passed through the filter of religious belief, and the rejection of progressive change is then based on faith alone. Routinely, the thinking that influences the religious is harshly opposed to change—even when the change can be called indispensable progress, and the benefits to the human condition are indisputable. History has many illustrations of resilient and passionate opposition to scientific discoveries initiated by diverse religious clusters. Let us recall the astronomical discoveries from past centuries that, in fact, discovered that the world is not the center of the universe. The religious person believed and enjoyed the concept that he or she, along with his or her God, is the center of everything, including the universe. Dislocating man from his sacred and significant place could not be easily allowed; he or she was fighting furiously against any attempt, scientific or not, to be dislocated. Violence and killing of scientific heretics was the means of purging the world of the bad news messengers—the bad news that man and his or her planet are not as he or she liked them to be.

Yes, the scientific discoveries are, at times, not welcome when the news is not pleasant or helpful. One must be a delude not to accept the scientific truth, sometimes the damning truth, regardless of the unwanted implications it brings. By rejection of the complicated science that led to the discovery and also by fallacious *ad hominem* attacks against its messengers/the scientists, the deluded fools are shielding themselves from news they dislike. At times, the uncertainty and also the opposed opinions of scientists regarding same matter are a source of great pleasure and the opportunity to choose a side that fits the fool's careless opinion. Deludes do not embrace the scientific or political reality. They like their world to remain as they perceive it, and therefore, they can differentiate as strict political conservatives, for example.

Particular social habits are responsible for creating mass actions: such as the criminal version of some acts that has sprung from irrational religious exaggerations and interpretations. Western cultures have created a tolerance for acts of discrimination, abuse, and oppression of groups of people branded suspect/inferior. There is a tendency of rigidity and prejudgment of social sections without any regard to the official and well-promoted value of liberty, dignity, and civil rights. The anti-violent/criminal opinion is so strong that even pets are required, against their natural instincts, to be non-aggressive or to meet self-destruction even when under unbearable stress. It is not the pet's need that is protected but the slaughter of the pet that is a consequence of the society that cannot tolerate easily acts of violence—a society that has become violent itself in the classification of caring.

A delude has his or her own original opinion about generally everything and, in particular, to controversial social dilemmas such as homosexuality. Homosexuality is a form of sexuality, a form fulfilling strong sexual desires; however, it is not in a traditional, heterogeneous way. The strong sexual desires and pleasures associated with the sexual act are a consequence of the specie's essential requisite of procreation. This intense desire was biologically formed and intended to improve the odds for the specie's perpetuation. In both the heterogeneous and homosexual relations, the aim of the relationship is in many ways similar. The difference is that in a man/woman relationship, the intended natural component of sexual intercourse, the prospect of procreation, is preserved. Therefore, in heterogeneous relationships, sexual activity has a dual meaning, while in the case of homosexuality, the procreation component is missing. In the heterogeneous act, there are all sorts of artificial and medical avenues in the search to avoid the procreation component, for strong pleasurable experiences are simply the ones sought after. An addiction to the frequent sexual thrill is mostly a norm and not an exception in modern societies.

In the past, even bestiality, humans having sex with some different specie's members, was recorded. It is said that the homosexual condition is not natural to the human condition, and it has the root in the habit, and perhaps in the addiction and the restless search for strong pleasure experiences. In particular cases it is a search for meaning or identity. For now, homosexual couples cannot form a traditional family; that is due to the fact that they cannot procreate, and the family they could generate would not contribute to our species' perpetuation. Perhaps the time will come when medical advances will make it possible for the genetic traits of a same-sex couple to be merged into the creation of an offspring. But at this time, that is just an idea that belongs to the imagined future even though this achievement will imply an asexual process, and the procreation component will again be absent as part of the sexual contact. Could a future homosexual family achieve to acquire its own biological children who can call themselves natural brothers and sisters? The union between man and woman, man and man, or woman and woman could be extended to any people in the society and for other reasons than satisfying sexual desires: such as financial or political benefit. If a deluded fool interacts with others in his or her neighborhood, then the caring that is asserted and implied confuses him or her. "You should love your neighbor" is a common saying, but the deluded fool loves his or her neighbor only in special conditions—for example, if he or she is sexually attractive.

The concept of marriage is not uniform among cultures or among religions. Some cultures allow only restrictive membership to marriage and families. The Western model that only a woman and a man form a marriage is the basis of a new family that has spread around the world, while only a few cultures allow for multiple members to join in one marriage. The Western cultures also allow, for example, a man to marry a number of wives; however, he may only do it in a succession that allows having one wife at a time, and a divorce of the previous wife must isolate the relationships. The divorce frequently calls for separating children from some of the parents or siblings, and in general, the divorce is a highly destructive and unnatural process. While some of the old ways of less restrictive marriage have their shortfalls, they seem to be able to support a more solid foundation for the institution we call here a family. As it is now, it seems that the base of what we now call marriage has many negative consequences, and it might, because of that, vanish in the future.

To feed someone and not respect him is as raising pigs; to love someone and not respect him is as keeping pets.

—MENCIUS.

A deluded fool occasionally likes pets: such as dogs and cats. Like most of us, he or she also loves the animals that live wild in a natural setting: such as deer or bears. In a deluded foolish view, the life of other animals is inferior, and he or she regards them as irrational. Most animals know fear—consequently anticipation—therefore, they are capable of rational thinking. Regarding the animal rights matter, the deluded fool acts in a way characteristic of his or her mental condition. He or she becomes resentful of the people that abuse animals, but he or she becomes careless, even violent, toward the animals when he or she follows some other need that is contrary to animal rights. The deluded fool is not a vegan,[35] and he or she can

---

35 *Vegan: a person who does not eat any animal products, including eggs and milk.*

hardly reconcile the need for meat as food or the accepted rights of animals. A delude is not a balanced person, and this logical conflict brings him or her to a condition of shameful confusion and erratic behavior.

Be kind, for everyone you meet is fighting a hard battle.

—PLATO

None of us like to have fake friends; it is better live alone than among adversaries. When the underlying reason for friendship is some sexual attraction, then you must agree that a sexual partner sees you as a body and not as an intellectual partner; that is probably not a genuine friendship. We, the humans, are social beings; that treatment is deeply embedded in our being. We have the natural desire to be together with others for no obvious reason. This necessity has perhaps developed over time; it has provided some comfort and safety during critical times. It is obvious that "one cannot break his own chains, but it can break the chains of his friend"—a practical and vital concept that would justify some reason for mutual friendship.

Yes, the delude does need a life partner, and sometimes he or she becomes successful. The marriage becomes a bridge between moral obligation and desirable pleasure; this can be mental or plain bodily pleasure. There is no real good in sexual pleasure, and a delude has no opportunity to understand the meaning of such a concept. The delude tries to cope with the new reality. For example, a marriage has its benefits. If he or she can hold a job, a carrier is not suitable for him or her; then things can become temporarily promising. His or her character does require much devotion, also respect, from his or her partner; but how can anyone respect a delude? For some, only certain financial means are available to achieve some form of happiness, and for some, it is the only thing; the material accumulation becomes their mighty desire. In this case, even the marriage becomes a business which must be properly managed by the selfish and appalling person—the fool.

Yes, the deluded fool loves freedom: the freedom to go undisturbed on his or her own desolate way.

~~~~~~

The whole problem with the world is that fools and fanatics are always so certain of themselves, but wiser people so full of doubts.

—BERTRAND RUSSELL

~~~~~~

For the deluded fool, happiness is to be found in pleasure or in what gives him or her pleasure. However, there is no genuine benefit in pleasure; only hard work commonly brings along material profit. And what do we do when we obtain some profit? Do we waste it to get some additional pleasure? Craving for money and riches is common for the foolish person, and this is far beyond the material things required for a comfortable or a worry-free life. By not being capable of grasping this truth, it provides him or her with a harsh way of universal disappointment and a means of self-destruction.

We all know that people are distinct and also, at the same time, similar; all have character traits we regard as positive or not. We can say that either all people are imperfect, or that all people are perfect in their own particular way. Not the deluded fool. He or she is assured that about everyone is undoubtedly less significant than he or she, which gives him or her unquestionable feeling of superiority. The deluded fool's pursuit for significance and comfort necessitate his or her search for synthetic aims to fulfill personal needs. If he or she can identify any means to reach his or her happiness, then he or she will seize coherent or fanatical measures to accomplish it. The exquisite projected look that style and fashion provide can offer some prospect for the delude to attain his or her wishes and provide him or her a way to put forward an undeniably unique personal statement. Some deluded fools are very much attracted by the fashion world, and, it seems for them, only appearance is important and allows him or her, with some advantage, to look down at the people who are not fashionable enough. In this case, the delude will spend endless hours and many available means to become vanguard fashionable.

Fashionable beauty is subjective. The belief that fashion is beautiful cannot be judged either true or false and therefore, becomes a private reputation. The subjective nature of fashion provides the delude a certain shield he or she needs to deflect attempts of judgment or doubt regarding his or her self-assured fashionably good taste. This is a powerful and profound way in which a delude achieves a clear status of superior and distinctive taste that he or she proudly and strongly extends to all other of his or her personality traits. As I mentioned earlier, a delude is not known to be balanced; extreme and mindless acts characterize his or her endeavors.

Humans are definitely social beings; they naturally thrive in communities. Most of the time a human community behaves like a bee hive, but at times also acts similar to a pack of angry wolves. The settled view is that friendships are natural and positive relationships among community members; they provide emotional support and boost an individual's meaning of happiness. When people, who are equal in most standards, establish mutual understanding, compassion, and trust toward each other, they originate an opportunity to become friends. Having no friends is considered personally and even socially harmful. Fake friends are useless. From a skeptical view, most happiness and almost all untested friendships are based on pure illusion; therefore, the real usefulness of such a relationship becomes a mirage and is insignificant. Most of the common people would naturally develop a number of friendships, with a few very close ones. This is somehow impossible for the delusional person due to the difficulty of reasonable understanding even of the basic requirements of such a relation. One component for the possibility of friendship is sharing similar views on diverse topics. The similarity of views will generate some agreement and solidarity that is paramount to a balanced relationship. Unfortunately, an unequal intellectual level, the *private context*,[36] and the different views of the same situation will generate disagreement that would be an obstacle in building a friendship relationship. Here is an example where there is a different view of some unique situation:

_____

36 *Private context: the totality of mental physical structures along with the memory objects accumulated by an individual.*

John Searle, a slusser professor of philosophy (text below), presented to us a polished and beautiful linguistic sentence, with precise structure and grammar, with regard to look at the mind compared with a computer program; writing is indicative of the reader's delight:

The reason that no computer program can ever be a mind is simply that a computer program is only syntactical, and minds are more than syntactical. Minds are semantical, in the sense that they have more than a formal structure, they have a content.

—JOHN SEARLE, *MINDS, BRAINS AND SCIENCE*

Here is a computer scientist's view/transformation:

The basis that no computer program can replicate a mind is basically that a computer program has a strict coding syntax grammar, while minds are more than syntactical. Minds enclose embedded meaning in addition to the logical structure in the sense that they possess more than a strict structure, they include data objects.

Now here is the fool's view:

All computers can not compare with the human mind; they are dumb. Computers do the thinking their own way; nevertheless, brains are smarter than the computer can ever be. The brains know a lot, because they remember what they learned.

These views, that describe the original Searle text and are intended to be similar in content, are distinct due to the *personal private mental context* of the readers. The private context determines the selection of specific words that would facilitate the translation of the identical text in conformity to the readers' way to understanding. The intended meaning of the text, subject of the transformation, is desired to be preserved. By deconstruction, a neutral view can detect components of the specific private context that is projected on the new form of the text presentation; it becomes a new view of the composition. To generalize this, even I know it is not advisable, the private mental context of individuals is essential for generating friendships, and opposing views of similar situations would become barriers in developing authentic closeness required for a genuine friendship.

Chapter 6

About Our Universe's Creation

People are many and diverse, and all, collectively, are what is called *humanity*. Humanity's search for understanding of our universe has included the exploration for the origin of our world and for the *Creator* of our universe. Religion identifies the Creator by many names: God, Buddha, Allah, Baha, and so on, with the note that most religions envision the Creator as a singular entity. From a transcendental argument of the existence of the Creator to the religious belief of pious human behavior as required by the Creator's revelations is a long way.

No human thing is of serious importance.

—Plato

For the most part religions have their structure rooted in miracles, myths, superstition, or indisputable belief. All this confirms and reinforces the patterns of a traditional religion. They also stimulate the imagination, invalidate the gap between a dream and actuality, and provide a small opening to a mystical world inhabited by the gods, the dead, and the spirits.[37] The pursuit for understanding the nature of the Creator has taken metaphysical or spiritual pathways, sometimes ignoring, or even rejecting, the proper scientific evidence that is also essential for a sound understanding.

At times, the ritualistic approach of discovery shifts to a metaphysical form of enquiry regarding the Creator, and that implies a transcendental extension of the intellect toward the concept of infinity, which is obviously impenetrable. Because of that, the metaphysical path to discover our Creator is unmanageable. Hitherto, the relation with the Creator was based mostly on the mystical spirituality of religion that was not restricted by the boundaries that lead to magical or metaphysical consideration of the Creator. Be not deceived, even what is regarded as magic conforms to the laws of nature, even when understanding of the way is unidentified. From the point of scientific method, we have difficulties in establishing the nature of the Creator, while the sound integration of mysticism, metaphysics, and science seems to be residing only in the realm of imagination.

Here we must admit that true religion is a very private and personal experience aiming at harmony and the complete truth, and it can become a personal and intimate path toward the search for the wisdom and the spirit of the Creator. At times, humanity accepts a religion that is unmistakably in contradiction to the scientific fact that leads to an erroneous interpretation of the Creator's nature. Some religious divides were not merely restricted to the members of a single group but were expanded against entire countries or, inward, have been extended across the threshold of homes, setting families against each other—even placing father against son or mother against daughter. Particular groups tried to gather all humanity to join in their religion, while other religions were on the path of annihilation of anyone who did not share their views.

---

37 *Mircea Eliade, 1951.*

We must state now that a number of religious groups have unfortunately chosen a long path that undertakes them further and further from the legitimate way of getting to apprehend and achieve closeness to the wisdom required to understand our Creator. In the search for our Creator, we must, in addition to religious revelation, follow the path of logical and scientific discovery; that will provide for us the eternal legitimate and complete truth concerning the nature of the creation. By abandoning logical inquiry, our search can wander in the deep darkness of illusion that takes us further and further from our purpose. This is what the deluded fool commonly does.

There are many paths to the top of the mountain, but the view is always the same.

—ASIAN PROVERB

As Saint Augustine distinctively articulated, an interpretation of religious wisdom must be revised when it confronts properly formulated scientific knowledge. This is especially valid when a new scientific paradigm emerges: this requires that the previous scientific learning be revised or even discarded. Hitherto, scientific wisdom has been volatile, and that is a justified reason for the religious doctrine to remain unwavering—in the hope that new scientific discovery will reconcile with the religious way. In some particular cases, we must discard proven scientific wisdom that is well connected to rationality to allow for dogmatic religious belief; this is not a true religious belief but the belief of the deluded fool. Any true religious belief is required to satisfy the requirement of rational thinking. A logical contradiction with physical reality provided by our senses indicates that we deviated from the right path of discovering the Creator and we now follow the deluded fools' way.

It is self-evident that when we grasp that our understanding of the universe amounts to about nothing, then, in fact, we know something. We say that the universe started from *nothing*—the creation *ex nihilo*. Nothing itself is impossible not to exist; the concept of nothing is at least a word. In mathematics, the representation of nothing is zero; zero is a number, a part of the foundation of mathematics. *'Nothing'* is not a number, is it a part of the reality? Can *nothing* exist as itself and be more than a word? In this context, *nothing* may point only to physical matter, or may possibly include a spiritual component as well? The creation of the material universe from nothing implies that the Creator does not meet our usual physical anticipation, and that it existed beyond the concept of nothingness, and it must have existed in an immaterial state only (spiritual) if the Creator's existence is to be logically justified. If our Creator formed all the fundamental material particles from his action alone, then the Creator cannot be material unless he created himself as well. To support an argument that the universe was created, we must accept that the universe cannot be infinite unless we accept that the Creator also created itself, and it is part of the universe that was created.

Can matter be created by action alone or by some action that springs from an immaterial cause? In Einstein's famous formula, $e=mc^2$, there is a direct equality relationship between matter and energy. Can we infer that matter can emerge from nothing else but energy alone? The light ray, due to its dual characteristics, seems to be a link that can connect the non-material world/energy with the material one. We can also question if the Creator is a being or a magnificent process. Some hypotheses forward the opinion that the universe was created by the *big bang* and that the expansion of the universe is presently ongoing. This theory is based on the former existence of a dense singularity and its expansion that has created some cosmic object that we call universe. Nevertheless, the singularity by itself can be seen as the *universe* itself; its expansion is a transformation, a change, to the state of the universe and not an act of creation. If we indeed exist, consequently, the Creator of our universe exists but not in a strict interpretation that stems from a narrow interpretation of the universe or the Creator; that has as its basis in imagination, fear, or downright ignorance.

There was a need for the Creator's acknowledgement as the originator of the universe. If the Creator is eternal, the universe, the Creator's work, is not guaranteed to be eternal as well. The famous Saint Anslem's sentence, "that than which nothing greater can be conceived, " incorporates the vast unknown in human understanding; therefore, the unknown is attributed to the Creator. One common concept also satisfies the Saint Anslem's sentence, and that is the widely used concept of infinity. There is nothing greater than infinity, nothing more mysterious than the infinite space or time, and nothing more mysterious than the Creator. In this way, it seems that there is a symbolic correlation connecting the concept of infinity and the transcendental vision of the mighty Creator. It is undoubtedly beyond human capabilities to comprehend the vast complexity of our universe from our remote place in the galaxy. We must follow the universal laws of nature and learn what is possible about our world. Finding the Creator's place in our universe can be revealed to us by careful attention to our world: using the power of our mind and origin in our endeavor of scientific discovery and logic.

Is life in our solar system self-contained, or is it part of the life present in the entire universe? The distance between stellar systems is immense. This would deter earth-like life forms from spreading among cosmic objects and make it nearly unattainable for the life forms that exist on our planet to propagate and continue their existence in the other part of the universe. The conditions that originated the emergence of life in our solar system are probable to be general in the entire universe. Therefore, the conditions for initiating life are present universally. Here we assume that every small part of the universe represents the properties of the entire universe, and that is not a guaranteed generalization. Is the duration of creation small or about instant or does it imply some duration? The creation of life might not be on an interval scale easily comprehended by us, the humans. In fact, the creation of life on earth might not be yet completed, and our struggle to understand our imperfections is just our absence of understanding the facts about this event. Potentially, our solar system was created directly by the Creator; however, the emergence of life happened much later and was independent of the original system's creation; that was due to the intrinsic properties and qualities of our solar system. The theory of evolution hypothesizes that life evolved from some previous condition to some new and improved biological structure. The theory of evolution does not apply to material or lifeless objects and does not account for the change from an inert material state to the new condition of life.

Creation is not evolution. Creation implies changes from the inert physical material form to a new state—the life form. Life could not begin its evolution if it was not first created, and therefore, both theories are valid, even though the mystery of the creation processes is not agreeably comprehended yet. Furthermore, can the evolution be an afterward stage of the initial creation process, and therefore, the creation is still ongoing? From the initial stage of life creation, there is a long road and there must be mysterious transformations before arriving at the life form we call a human being. Perhaps it is improper to say, but evolution has been observed also in the case of technological progress. Most new products are an improvement (an evolution) with regard to the previous version. For example, computers are continuously improving the performance of the new released models, and that can be characterized as technological evolution. The Second Law of Thermodynamics simply asserts that entropy in a system increases with time, I wonder if evolution is factually a path to introduce unmanageable complexity in a system and therefore, a component that leads to unsuspected obliteration.

To apprehend the universal truth, the intellect must possess infinite power since it extends its understanding from the particular to the infinite. That is not credibly possible, and it raises uncertainty regarding our limits toward the prospect of consistent sound understanding. The uncertainty is not about the Creator's obligatory nature but about the Creator's questionable actuality. Could the universe self-create itself from nothing and not be assembled from matter already created? There is no doubt that the Creator is in harmony with his own creation. Also, the Creator is in harmony with the laws of nature and with scientific discovery—things that the Creator itself established. Also, we must acknowledge that our physical world, the object of the Creator's accomplishment, cannot be eternal in this state as the view that nothing is permanent but change itself is widely accepted.

In various religions, the wisdom regarding the Creator's revelation is found in holy books that are translated in numerous languages. Jacques Derrida's deconstruction concept affirms that we routinely dismantle some text and then reconstruct it ourselves in a new personal context. In this way, the translation becomes merely a personal interpretation. Even more, deconstruction denies the possibility of an exact translation due to the dualistic hierarchies embedded in the original version of the text, and therefore, much meaning is lost in the translated books. This is a very serious and unresolved religious matter. A committed effort toward the rigorous analysis of the literal meaning of a text and also the search for hidden meaning in the neglected parts of the text sometimes point toward discovery of alternate new meanings. Often the detail that is found (and the meaning of it) gains more significance than the full text that also incorporates the detail and gains illogical meaning when isolated from the context in which its meaning was created. At times, text meanings are potentially veiled under the metaphorical attribute of the text and are not logically sound as direct literary translations. It is no wonder that various religious believers travel to the original place of initiation of a religious faith. Being in the original location of the religious acts must be comforting, and it also places the believer in the true spatial context of the religious act; it helps acquire a better understanding and provides avoidance of the wrong meaning or interpretation. Pilgrimages to holy sites have a deep and true meaning and are essential for the genuine religious experience.

By discovering his or her power of the intellect, man or woman placed himself or herself as a grandiose focal point of the universe— as the greatest creation of our Creator. For any man or woman, any point could be viewed as a center of the earth; likewise, to any observer at sea, the horizon seems to be equally distant in all directions, regardless of the position of observation. Looking around on a starry night, we might have the feeling that the distance is even in all directions and we are in the middle, in the center, of the cosmic space. Any exploration must have a starting point for any spatial orientation, and that is why our planet is the origin in all our exploration—either religious or scientific. For the profane, perhaps the realization of the *big bang* has provided a new special point as the center of our expanding universe, while the center of our inquiry and exploration retains its start from our planet—a place long established in our experiences. Therefore, the concept that man or woman is in the center of the universe is potentially valid and based on our deeply entrenched view of the world. In that regard, we must declare that the man or woman, his or her planet, and the world are forever situated as our point of origin toward the mysterious space.

Regardless of how long the path toward finding out about the Creator, the scope of the travel is to discover the true nature of the universe creation. It is also obvious that man cannot discover the act of creation unless it is so desired and allowed by the Creator. Is the struggle among religions an attempt to prove that the only path to the Creator is by following their own distinct ways? It is not appropriate to say that "only one road leads to Rome" when we know the metaphor is that "all roads lead to Rome." In the same way, all religions anticipate understanding of the Creator. We can imagine an invisible man; the invisible cannot be perceived by our external visual sense, but it can be sensed by the mind. The invisible man is not an innate idea, and it has its roots in the external and also the internal mental world of the mind. The invisible man is a man and also has the attribute of not being detected by our vision senses; however, it is possible that it can be distinguished by hearing, touching, etc. If it cannot be detected by all external senses, then can we call it reality? Some entities, as the Creator is, are detected only by the cognitive qualities of the mind alone and are not detected by our external sensual perceptions. How can we be sure that the Creator is, when we are required to detect reality by the use of our external senses? Is the contrary also true that we can detect an object by our senses, while the mind refuses to acknowledge its existence?

We also must agree that, at times, we assume that what we can't perceive does not exist: a dog with five legs, for example. We certainly can't see electricity, but we must admit its existence by its cause-and-effect connecting principle. We can state that the Creator has not been an entity possible to be sensed as a perception, or we, the humans, could not identify such an occurrence. The Creator can be defined as an objective truth reflected by the power of the mind. Unless we accept the mind itself as a way for some inferred sensual perception, we must agree that the Creator is not perceivable by our senses.

Some religions have their foundation on strict interpretation of religious doctrines that base their judgment on inflexible opinions which are contrary to any formal way of judgment, illogical, and unmistakably outside scientific thought. This is the common condition associated with the deluded fools' religion—a religion that can be in deep conflict with common law and scientific principles. One of the universal misunderstandings is that some heretics suppose that scientific inquiry is not, and cannot be, a legitimate religious activity. To assume infinite power to the Creator is a simple solution and provides an answer to every question or unknown thought about our world. It is a very simple and convenient way to reduce all inquiries of everything, including the unknown, to an irrefutable belief or justification.

From a transcendental argument of the existence of the Creator to the religious belief of pious human behavior as required by the Creator, it is a long way that cannot be followed on a rational route. Does religion emerge from the transcendental capability of human mind? True happiness lies in what is eternal; therefore, the search for happiness can lead us to acceptance of the promise for eternal life. I tie the concept of the existence of the Creator with an assumption of our wishful desire for eternal life. Is seeking the eternal life by our religious belief an attempt to gain independence from the cruelty of time? How is a human to live in a world dominated by chaos, suffering, and absurdity without the hope for guaranteed future tranquility? Therefore, the concept of heaven was necessary as a place where happiness is to be realized and where eternal life is not only possible, but it is also a promise.

No testimony is sufficient to establish a miracle, unless the testimony is of such a kind, that its falsehood would be more miraculous than the fact that it endeavors to establish.

—DAVID HUME, *AN ENQUIRY CONCERNING HUMAN UNDERSTANDING*

My grandmother Maria, a person of whom I have memories that I deeply cherish, told me that during a storm fish and frogs were falling from the sky along with the rain. She asked me not to share this with others out of concern that I would become a target of ridicule since the fact was not believable. Was this a miracle? Even though this story can be seen as doubtful, I have not questioned the truth of the matter. After a few years and some reflection, I became aware again of her story, and I came to a possible logical explanation: some tornado/twister might have been the cause of the fish being lifted from a pond and moved to the atmosphere, and later, they were falling down in a distant place. I am wondering at the concept of a miracle. We may regard a highly unusual event a miracle when we have difficulties in arriving to the proper understanding of its cause?

The Christian religion not only was at first attended with miracles, but also even at this day cannot be believed by any reasonable person without one.

—DAVID HUME, *AN ENQUIRY CONCERNING HUMAN UNDERSTANDING*

The need for the existence of the Creator as the initiator of the entire universe perhaps started as a sensible idea meant to provide the need for particular understanding of the universe—a task that probably greatly surpasses our natural abilities. Yes, we need an undeniably good answer for all creation questions about the unknown, and a way is to assign it to the all-powerful Creator. The deluded fool's unquestioned belief in the absolute correctness of his or her inflexible religious beliefs, and therefore a personal view of the Creator, can come near a state of mental incapacitation: in other words, a borderline mental disorder.

From a skeptical view, some hypothesis of the creation of the universe transcends and rejects the materialistic perspective, and that is called faulty science. Some religions assume that the Creator is presently and closely involved in the activities of our personal lives. The skeptic can reasonably doubt the Creator's involvement in our private life by pointing out that all the prayers in the world can't *crack a nut,* or that the Creator can easily transform a boat into a house but is not known to have ever done so. If the Creator did not like the people of the world, he has the power to send misfortune and destroy them. But it does not; there are many people all over the world. That alone is enough proof that the Creator loves the humanity he created—if he is as envisioned by various religions.

In our imaginations, fantasies, or dreams we can regard ourselves as the most important creation of the Creator—a selfish and perhaps arrogant belief however, an eternal component of human existence. The earth has not ended with the stop of some forms of life—as the dinosaur's existence—but has changed along with other forms of life and other species. Now the human is the dominant species on earth; however, there is no guarantee that the future holds a place for human life on earth, and we should not imply that humans are a necessary species for life on earth to persist. It might be the other way, for the life on our planet to continue the human race is obligatory to become extinct.

We can't deny the possibility of anything justifying that on skepticism alone. From only a materialistic point, the creation of the universe is unfeasible to validate, and therefore, the need to allow other theories is necessary.[38] To be valid, a theory about the creation of universe must be anchored in the space of natural sciences; it must exit the metaphysical space, and must be confined to the predictable view of scientific discovery. Furthermore, any theory for the creation of universe must satisfy the necessities of the *reasoned fact* paradigm and also the materialistic view of the *matter of fact;* otherwise, it must be discarded, as we have no valid logical ground to initiate our judgment. Before we accept a theory for the creation of the universe, we must eliminate any conflict between empirical observations and the logical component.

---

38 *Materialism asserts that matter cannot be created from nothing; however, materialistically, a new form of matter is merely a transformation. The emergence of matter only from energy alone does not satisfy the materialistic paradigm.*

CHAPTER 7

The Soul and Genetics

oul—in the Greek language, it is a word that distinguishes the living body from inanimate matter. Platonists say that man or woman is a soul using a body rather than a composite of the soul and body. The inference of this is that the nature of man or woman originates wholly in the soul, and that the body is just a temporary dwelling. Plato struggled to guard the purity of comprehensible essences—universality, and the nonmaterial component of intellectual awareness—as well as the sensible dignity of the soul from the *blemish* of the material world.

Death may be the greatest of all human blessings.

—SOCRATES

An empirical investigation of the soul is not anticipated as possible. Does a simple or do several complex concepts fit better the description of the soul? Can the soul be a stream, the functionality of a body that is immortal, and be transmitted from a body to another thru gestation and procreation? If the soul emerges at the birth of a human being, an appropriate question is about who gave life to the first human being? It sounds absurd, but if the first human being was born and therefore had a mother, then it could not possibly be the first human being; unless the mother was a non-human. Can the soul enjoy absolute freedom locked in its physical body? When we say that after the dissolution of the body the ego is annihilated, perishes, and does not exist after death, is that acceptable to satisfy our personal ego? Is the emergence of the soul concept a justification or denial of such a meaningless outcome?

And some women, like the females of other animals, for example mares and cows have a strong tendency to produce offspring resembling their parents.

—ARISTOTLE, *POLITICA*

It is reasonable to believe that Socrates and Plato have noted similarity of distinct human beings and also the inheritance of some properties that have been exported from parents to their offspring. This inheritance can be easily clarified now by genetics. The veiled mystery of human genetics is likely partially accountable for the emergence of the soul concept. The results of the genetic mechanism are easily identified, while the intricacy of genetics is still far from being well understood. Was, in fact, Socrates so confident of the existence of the soul that perhaps it made him give up his life with the conviction that life is, in fact, eternal, and conceivably, death is only a transformation and a blessing? Socrates, and also Plato, believed that life and even consciousness persists after the body has perished. It is implicit that the soul does not necessitate a material body to exist, and it departs the body at the end of the existence of life. Does the soul, after it leaves the body, become some sort of an angel? In the dogmatic expectation of religions, the body will return to nature, by discomposing, and the soul will rise to the heavens and be eternal. Because of this, the soul should be infinitely more important than that of the temporal body.

How can the increased number of immortal souls be explained in the case of the large population growth? A number of new souls are to be created, the same soul might populate numerous bodies, or there is no good explication or explanation to account for this circumstance. Is it then reasonable to assume that, as a matter of fact, souls cannot factually exist, or that a soul is as fire: once started, it spreads itself and moves itself to a new medium? How can we justify the disappearance of the souls of the dinosaurs, or are the dinosaur souls still presently lingering around in the bodies of today's life forms?

There is a correlation between the soul and genetics. We cannot account for our changes to adapt to our environment any other way than by the theory of evolution and the export of gained biological improvements by genetic processes. Certainly, the theory of evolution cannot account for the beginning of life. The soul is similar to a spark: in one instance, it ignites life in a new body; this is at the time of conception. At some point, the soul is unable to subsist in the inadequate body; the body then becomes lifeless again, in a material-only state, and returns to the inert physical state of nature. This is similar to a radio that comes to life when the stream of electrical power is allowed to travel to its circuits and actualize its functionality—an abstract form of life—or later becomes silent (lifeless) when the power is interrupted.

The connection between the soul and genetics is apparent, and we can assert that the *soul*'s emergence concept is embedded in the genetic construction of a being. The genetic construction is changing in time, and the possibility of life emergency by soul actualization is not, therefore, guaranteed. Is there a possibility of changes in the genome construction of a being to deny the soul the possibility and actualization of becoming a living being? The modern human changes and the environment that he or she lives might be changing faster than the body can improve and adapt to. What if *genetics* falls behind and is no longer able to correct or improve the subject to the faster changing environment? Is there a limit for the physical body in its chance and its ability to adjust to the changing external environment? In what condition can the body no longer adjust to the change?

Genetics promotes the change in a person, and that change can be later passed on to a future offspring. The amount of change is incredibly small, and the new change requirements are so dynamic that sensible genetic changes are no longer possible. Is genetics able to improve the future physical body to the changes in the environment that have destroyed its ancestral source? Can they continue from any point in the development line? Can the rate of change, faster than the human body can handle, be a source for its annihilation or destruction of the species? Some genetic changes must be unlearned and rolled back to some old patterns and conditions once it is destructive to continue on the current biological path. Biological enhancement provided by genetics is not an accident, but it is a necessity for the required correction to adhere to the biological need of the ever-changing natural settings in which life flourishes. Slowing down the change in our natural existence setting is perhaps required for the future survival of our species. Our technological progress facilitated the forceful environmental changes. It is now beyond the capacity of our genetic mechanism to forwardly adjust to it and to possibly find a means to correct it.

As it is sensibly expected, a delude hastily rejects the complex intricacy of the genetic process. It is better suitable for him to embrace simpler concepts such as reincarnation: the spiritual rebirth of the soul in a different new body. This can provide elucidation for sharing and propagating the physical and spiritual characteristics that are common among the related members of a family or group. This accounts for the existence of absolute similarities of character or physical appearance without having the need for the existence of the reality of genetic processes. The soul is held to be perpetual, with occasional descent into the state of material existence and absorbed in the illusion of some recompense possible only in the reality of the physical world. The delude sees no difficulty in accepting the doctrine of reincarnation, even when, at times, this includes the passage of the soul into a non-human—into an animal body. The concept of reincarnation offers the opportunity for a connection from pure spiritualism mode to inert physical matter.

At times, reincarnation is seen as superstition, and in that setting, it is appropriately regarded only as an unscientific concept. The belief in reincarnation has ancient roots. The idea thrived mainly in Oriental cultures and later was entertained by some in the West. Popular Hinduism conveys that the soul is repetitively passed from one physical body to a new one through the physical cycle of death and birth. The rebirth and reincarnation is done because of desire: a soul wishes to be reborn to fulfill his or her desire for worldly pleasures, which can only be enjoyed by populating a physical body. The delude is readily disposed to embrace the religious belief that the soul will be held accountable and subject to judgment and even punishment after the body is dead; this occurs along with the promise of the eternal possibility for existence after physical life existence. One view is that the soul's qualities are spread in a pool along with the traits of other souls; the new soul's characteristics are constructed from a set of the traits of this pool that later come into physical reality in new reincarnations.

The progress in the scientific understanding of the human being has provided much insight regarding the human condition, and has provided an alternative basis for what inductively lead to the emergence of the concept of the soul. Now, the concept of the soul does not require travel in the world of imagination and synthetic reasoning. The soul can be seen as the spiritual, indispensable component of the human being—a component that separates us from the inert physical state and that accounts for our feelings, emotions and desires that cannot be justified by the properties of physical matter alone. Certainly, the definition of the soul must be revised to include new scientific discoveries, and some details, as the concept of reincarnation must be perhaps discarded. As David Hume noted that the future is the projection of the past, and as human develops, it is predictable. Humans have not changed much in the last thousand years. For example, how can one say that he is a better man than Aristotle?

The ancient Chinese Dao philosophy entails the concept that the human body vanishes and dissolves like everything else in the infinite process of change—a fact not probable to be ever refuted.

Envisioned this way, the destruction of the body, as the destruction of the entire universe, becomes simply a transformation. Also, new scientific theories seem to erase the divide between material and energy or conceivably spiritual objects; the fundamental physical matter itself is now understood as a mere pattern of vibration. That would close the theoretical gap between what the body and soul are, and reincarnation may merely mean that multiple beings could be constructed from the same elementary particles—but at different times.

Related Essays
and
Quotations

Philosophy is Dead

I was enthusiastically waiting for the release of the new book, *The Grand Design*, a writing coauthored by the venerated Stephen Hawking and Leonard Mlodinow. To my amazement, on the first page of the new book the authors make a shocking statement about the state of philosophy: *"Traditionally these are questions for philosophy. But philosophy is dead. Philosophy has not kept up with modern development in science, particularly physics."* I assumed that philosophy was alive and well—what happened?

Let's *deconstruct* the second sentence to expose the possibility of a potential alternate meaning. If we replace the word *philosophy* with its classical vocabulary meaning, *love of wisdom,* the sentence becomes: *Love of wisdom has not kept up with modern development in science, particularly physics*. In this way it looks as if the scientific way of physics has abandoned the proper logical development path—bizarre. That is an old, known state of affairs, and we must regretfully agree that both the philosophy and scientific history are packed with instances of countless erroneous theories. We can reasonably affirm that this unfortunate situation continues at the present time.

Over time, the development of philosophy was carried on parallel with other scientific discoveries or the progress of other numerous fields of knowledge. Philosophy tends to analyze some general event and searches for a simplified explanation to describe it, to narrow it down, or to clarify its meaning. This is the reverse of pure mathematics, which commonly begins with a definition or axiom that is built upon to generate some new and complex logical structure. It is then obvious that the methods and requirements of philosophy are not similar to those of some other scientific methods, and here is where the divide may possibly originate. It is now generally agreed that it is not possible any longer—due to the enormous amount of the collected scientific data and the complexity of the subject—for common humans to follow and understand the entire thought processes of modern theoretical scientific development. More and more, the attention to detail and worry is essential to not abandon the rational/scientific path for the mysterious and synthetic way of unsound thinking.

Sound thinking would imply that we hold our opinion if we don't grasp enough insight regarding the subject examined; any expressed opinion about the subject would be a waste. We must note here that even a generally accepted opinion can be mistaken; also, an abstract syllogism definitely does not guarantee a unique conclusion. Various assumptions are imaginary and arbitrary deceptions, rooted in the intrinsic abstract ability of the mind. Scientific knowledge, in particular, ought not to be based on theory alone—even if later the scientific concept is to be proven accurate. We tend to look for formulas and observations to support our promoted assumptions only, and we neglect, or sometimes even discard, valid observations that seem, at first, to contradict our vague understanding. We ought to have confidence only in what is completely known and is not possible to be doubted. All scientific knowledge is required to conform to the precise methods of mathematics and logic, or to be a consequence of consistent empirical observations.

As Thomas Kuhn warned us in his work, *The Structure of Scientific Revolutions,* from time to time, scientific thought is prone to change due to the emergence of a new scientific paradigm. These are new paradigm shifts to new approaches to proper understanding that scientists have ignored or have not considered earlier as legitimate. When scientists spend an staggering effort in attempting to enlarge the central paradigm by merely applying sophisticated and un-provable theories that *fit* the observed data points, then we likely approach the threshold that will generate the surge toward a new paradigm.

The discussed book clearly is a profound statement regarding the state of our part of the universe and the realization that physical laws alone could justify the emergence of our galactic system. Because our galactic object that originated from the initial *big bang* is currently expanding—and that implies a border condition—and also had a location of origin that we can call *center*, it does not fit the philosophical definition of an infinite object. In my understanding, an infinite object cannot have a center or boundaries, even if the details of the expanding border are unknown. We have applied the mathematical abstraction view of infinity to physical objects with the omission to observe that abstractions are outside the field of real-time or actual physical space. We found out that our galactic *object* does not fit the definition of the word *universe*. We could find a new name for it—something like *big stellar*—and leave the concept of the universe intact.

There is no harm in the will to understand as long as it is recognized that knowledge and the entire truth are beyond the humans' natural abilities to comprehend. Is there any knowledge in the world which is so perfect that a reasonable man could not ever doubt it? In my view, the statement that philosophy is somehow dead is regrettable and must be looked at as an imprudent attempt to *slaughter* it. People have changed: we no longer visit a barbershop to have our teeth extracted, we do not pray for the rain to come. We live in a new world, and sometimes we are not aware that philosophy itself has progressed immensely in the last century—especially the subject has become unfamiliar to individuals that are immersed in their own overwhelming scientific subject.

Disjoint Points of Reference

Various contemporary arguments end with floods of raw emotions and disregard of reason; several social, environmental, animal rights, or nationalistic views seem irreconcilable. The familiar fallacies—such as false dilemma, irrelevant conclusion, false cause, and *red herring*—offer a partial view on the falsity of the premises and do not lead to the construction of a sound syllogism.

Let us begin with an abstract view of life on our planet, the human's place on this earth, and the requirements and obstacles for our preserving its life. Life on earth has not ended with the extinction of some forms of life—such as dinosaurs—but it has changed. Other species—as humankind—have become the dominant species. Sometimes we, the humans, assume that God has created the entire world only for us. This is naïve, because the earth was great before man populated it, and it would still be great after the probable destruction of humans on the earth. We, the humans, are responsible for gross impact on nature, and we have been able to pollute the rivers, forests, and even oceans to a grim level. There is no guarantee that the future holds a place for human life on earth, and we have no justification to imply that humans are a necessary species for life on earth to continue. It might become necessary for the human race to become extinct so that other forms of life to continue on our planet.

We could become extinct as well, and become like the dinosaurs, former principal beings of the distant past.

Formerly, a difficulty appeared from faulty judgment, and disregard for the well-being of all God's creatures. These led to artificial and monstrous acts which, unfortunately, have been a common part of humanity. The today's world injustices, violence—even killings—are unacceptable, as all humans are, at least, creatures of the mighty God. We extend this injustice to the existence of animals, because they are also the creatures of God.

Also, it is known that people are, by their nature, obligated to self-defense and to the duty of race preservation; this is in the strictest way, and is not for artificial reasons based on one's false interpretation of natural order. Human understanding is limited by the power provided by the mind and by the short human lifespan, and also by the relentlessly present prejudices or bias. It is the mind power of the human that has inquired about the origin of our world, our life, and the universe; the search for the meaning is still ongoing. Men or women, therefore, may be called irrational if they allow their actions to be determined by morality. As Arthur Schopenhauer noted, moral law is conditional. According to Aristotle, there is a natural hierarchy of living beings. The different levels are determined by the abilities present in the beings due to their natures. Human beings are regarded superior to any other animals, because human beings have the capacity to use reason to guide their conduct, while, it is said, that animals lack this ability and must instead rely mainly on instinct.

The great uniformity among the actions of men is universally acknowledged.

—DAVID HUME

In all nations and ages, human nature remains about the same. We humans are mostly meat eaters and, sometimes, are savage beasts that are a few steps above the apes in the woods, as Arthur Nietzsche once said. Our powerful urge to preserve our own existence is contrary to the wish of radical defenders of the environment: the irremediable antagonism and conflict between the requirements and demands of human nature and the restrictions of what we call *civilization*—as Sigmund Freud noted. In the famous Chinese teaching, "*Don't do to others what you wouldn't like done to yourself,*" Confucius perhaps was not reflecting about the steamed piglet he had for dinner when he used the words *to others*. According to Sigmund Freud, what we call our civilization is largely responsible for our misery; we would be much happier if we gave it up and returned to the primitive conditions. However the mystery is simpler and the problem is a logical fallacy, using as premises disjointed points of reference when constructing the argument. The conflict between our natural needs, our acquired synthetic sensitivity, and generalization of our observations of all animals has created a contradiction that can be resolved only if our priorities are strongly defined and acted upon. Is eating lamb or is the perpetuation of the lambs' lives essential to our self-preservation as a species? Or is it the sheep population that matters? The answer is that none of the possible options are complete. Lamb is an important part of most humans' diets, but it is not, alone, essential to the survival of our species. In their need for self-preservation and survival, humans seem a selfish and cruel species. It is said, that when our vital necessities are satisfied, then we can become caring and perhaps even kind.

Philosophical Quotations

Ancient Quotations

The prosperity of a fool is a heavy burden to put up with. —Aeschylus

The desire for imaginary benefits involves the loss of present blessings. —Aesop

That if anything is possible to inferior, weaker, and stupider people, it is more so for their opposites. —Aristotle

Delight, or the judgment or the lust of pleasure, destroys the judgment of prudence. —Aristotle

For instance, the stone which by nature moves downward cannot be habituated to move upwards, not even if one tries to train it by throwing it up ten thousand times. —Aristotle

People form true opinions, but because of their moral badness sometimes they do not say what they really think. —Aristotle

Others might equal his intelligence, but not equal his stupidity. —Confucius

Be not ashamed of mistakes and thus make them crimes. —Confucius

When I told him one thing he understands ten. —Confucius

Once harm has been done, even a fool understands it. —Homer

Ignorance — the root and the stem of every evil. —Plato

Wise men talk because they have something to say; fools, because they have to say something. —Plato

Any man can make mistakes, but only an idiot persists in his error. —Cicero

Classic Quotations

Of all thieves fools are the worst; they rob you of time and temper. —Goethe

A stupid man's report of what a clever man says can ever be accurate, because he unconsciously translates what he hears into something he understands. —Bertrand Russell

Deficiency in judgment is just what ordinarily is called stupidity, and for such a failing there is no remedy. —Immanuel Kant

Many assumptions are imaginary and arbitrary inventions of our mind. —Rene Descartes

Man is at bottom a savage, horrible beast. We know it only in the business of taming and restraining him, which we call civilization. Hence it is that we are terrified if now and them his nature breaks out. But it is unnecessary to wait for anarchy in order to gain enlightenment on this subject. A hundred records, old and new, produce the conviction that in his unrelenting cruelty man is in no way inferior to the tiger and the hyena. —Arthur Schopenhauer

Many people would sooner die than think. In fact they do. —Bertrand Russell

Delight in misfortune of others remains the worst trait of human nature. —Arthur Schopenhauer

In the part of this universe that we know there is great injustice, and often the good suffer, and often the wicked prosper, and one hardly knows which of those is the more annoying. —Bertrand Russell

Glossary

of

Philosophical Terms

A priori – a proposition is knowable *a priori* if it is knowable independently of experience.

An objection – a premise contrary to a premise.

An enthymeme – a syllogism starting from probabilities or signs.

Primary premise – a basic truth.

Basic truth – does not require a demonstration.

Axiom – basic truth named *par excellence*.

Definition – a thesis.

Absolutism – assumes that there are no restrictions on the right and powers of government.

Absurd – a belief that is obviously unattainable.

Accidentalism – the flow of events is unpredictable.

Actualism – also known as actual idealism — implies that only the actual world is real.

A fortiori – even more so.

Agnosticism – the view that some proposition is not known, and perhaps cannot be known to be true or false, usually applied to theological doctrines.

Anarchism – a view that human communities can and should flourish without government.

Anguish – in Sartre, an inescapable sense of deep and total responsibility for one owns choice and action.

Atrophic principle – if it would not exist we would not have talked about.

Antithesis – Greek – set against, in materialism the reaction to a change or process.

Antonym – a word of opposite meaning — e.g. real/unreal, good/bad.

Apathy – a worldly interest small or unworthy.

Apodictic – a necessarily true, or provable, or possessing certainty beyond dispute.

Arrow's theorem – logic of social choice and voting.

Auto logical – a word that applies to itself: 'short' is a short word, 'English' is an English word.

Beetle in a box – a probabilistic look at its containment.

Canonical – a canonical description of a sentence would be one that revealed its basic structure, or showed how the sentence is built by transformation from a basic structure.

Casualism – the doctrine that all things and events do not happen by chance.

Causation – central area of metaphysics. Causation is the relation between two events. That holds when, given that one occurs, it produces, or brings forth, or determines, or necessitates the second.

Central state materialism – identifies mental events, with physical events happening in the brain.

Change – a relationship of the change to time.

Chaos – the contrast between the ordered universe, and the undifferentiated beginnings of things.

Charisma – a charismatic leader exercise power thru quality apart from ordinary people, and becomes irrationally treated almost inhuman.

Closed formula – sentence, a formula in which all variables are bound.

Cognition – cognitive processes are those responsible for knowledge and awareness. They include the processing of experience, perception, memory, as well as overtly verbal thinking.

Conceive – to hold in the mind, or form the idea.

Conscience – an act of the consciousness human action that is morally required or forbidden.

Consciousness – it is the space where experiences and thoughts have their existence. Where our intentions are formed and desires are felt.

Corollary – a straightforward consequence of a theorem.

Creation ex nihilo – creation from nothing.

Cynic – a virtuous life that consists in independence achieved over one's desires and needs. Since one desires nothing, it lucks nothing.

Datum – evidence considered fixed for the purpose in hand.

Deconstruction – Derrida – a skeptical approach to coherent meaning, a contact with the external reality, or significance on a text.

Deceit – an intentional attempt to mislead people.

Defeasible – an opinion capable of being overturned by further events. At law, a judgment is defeasible, if can be overturned. A proposition is defeasible, if further evidence may render it doubtful.

Definist fallacy – the illicit insistence on defining a term in a way favorable to one's side of an argument.

Delude (noun) – an individual that is predisposed to develop illogical opinions of even the most elementary and basic events.

Delusion – holding a false opinion as truth despite overwhelming contrary evidence.

Democracy – Greek, rule by the people – the suzerainty of the people in general, expressed not directly by a vote, but by representative.

Democracy paradox – the obligation of the people to follow the majority decision with which he or she disagrees.

Deny – rejecting the request.

Deontological ethics – ethics based on the notion of duty.

Determinism – when every event has a cause.

Diachronic – Greek – through time, events of extended existence, contrasted with that of events (instantaneous).

Dialectic – the process of reasoning.

Disjoint – two sets are disjoint if they have no member in common.

Disjoint Points of Reference – dissimilar and independent views that aim at the same object or event.

Dogma – a belief held unquestionably with undefended certainty.

Doxa – Greek belief – an opinion contrasted with real knowledge in classical philosophy.

Dystopia – a negative utopia: place where all is not well.

Ecstasy – Greek – standing outside; a state in which normal sense experience is suspended or the subject is joyfully conscious of higher things.

Egoism – psychological egoism is the view that people are always motivated by self-interest.

Eidos – Greek form – abstract forms or ideas, term used by Plato.

Empathy – the state of being emotionally and cognitively 'in tune with' another person.

Entailment – a relationship between a set of premises and the conclusion, when the conclusion follows the premises.

Entrenchment – a predicate is entrenched if it is true as a matter of historical facts.

Entropy – a measure of disorder in a system.

Epistemology – the theory of knowledge.

Equivocate – to make a statement that is capable of being taken in more than one way, with the aim of exploiting the ambiguity.

Eristic – reasoning that aims not to truth, but at victory over an opponent or at making a weaker position prevail.

Essence – the basic or primary element in the being of a thing.

Eternity – the totality of time, conceived as having no beginning or end.

Event – a change or happening.

Evolution – a genetic transformation of populations thru time.

Exoteric – an opinion suitable for the uninitiated.

Foundationalism – the view in epistemology that knowledge must be regarded as a structure raised upon secure, certain foundation.

Freedom – negatively – is thought as an absence of constraint, and Hobbes say 'is the silence of the law'. Positively is a condition of liberation.

Functionalism – in philosophy of the mind, functionalism is the modern successor of behaviorism.

Fuzzy logic – a variant of set theory and logic that recognizes the degree of applicability of predicates.

Generative grammar – theory of languages published in 'Syntactic structures' the study of form of all possible human languages. The result will be a universal grammar.

Genetic fallacy – an argument rejected because its 'suspicious' origins.

Genome – the entire DNA content of an organism.

Genotype – an organism's genetic constitution.

Gnosis – Greek: knowledge – the root is found in agnosticism, diagnosis, and prognosis.

Hallucination – the occurrence of an experience in itself indistinguishable from a valid perception; however exists without an appropriate external cause.

Hell – a place reserved for unrepentant sinners after death, where they both suffer separation from God, and punishment.

Heuristic – a process, such as trial and error, for solving a problem for which no algorithm exists.

Homonyms – words that have same shape or form, but different meaning.

Hypothesis – proposition put forward as a supposition, rather than asserted.

Idealism – doctrine holding that reality is fundamentally mental in nature.

Immanent – operating from inside a thing or person; not external or transcendent.

Incongruent counterparts – spatial parts that related to each other as mirror images, have the same shape, but cannot super imposed as to occupy same space.

Inertial frame – reference for measurements of motion, space, and time.

Inference – the process from accepting of some proposition to some another.

Infinity – the unlimited that goes beyond any fixed bound.

Innate idea – ideas that are inborn, not a product of experience.

Instinct – innately and automated determined behavior, inflexible to change.

Intention – state of mind directed toward some state of affairs.

Interpretation – logic, informally an interpretation of a logical system assigns meaning or semantic value to the formulae and their elements.

Intuition – immediate awareness outside the control of deliberation and reason, regarded with suspicion.

Invalid – an argument is invalid when its conclusion does not follow from its premises.

Isomorphic – one to one representation between two systems.

Judgment – the affirmation of a judgment is thus the making of a true or false claim.

Law of effect – a view that actions that lead to immediate pleasure are remembered and repeated.

Lazy sophism – a line of reasoning leading to fatalism, and the consequent paralyses of action.

Lemma – an intermediate conclusion in a proof.

Lexeme – a word, in the sense as dictionary entry. Strings of letters might be forms of the same lexeme: fill, fillet, filling.

Lexical – is a way descriptive either of dictionaries, or the terms they are about.

Liberalism – the ideology of the individual thought of as possessing rights against the government, including the rights of equal respect, freedom of expression, freedom from religious and ideological constraint.

Lying – the deliberate utterance of a falsehood, with the intention to deceive or mislead.

Matter of fact – in Hume writing is the empirical things known by means of sense impressions.

Merit – some admirable qualities.

Misologists – those who do not like logical arguments.

Modality – the way a proposition is true or false.

Model – a set of sentences is an interpretation under which all are true.

Monism – it finds one when dualism finds two.

Moot – a disputation, a question is moot when still subject of a dispute is undecided.

Morpheme – the minimal unit of grammar.

Mysticism – a belief in union with divine nature by means of ecstatic contemplation, and access to knowledge closed off to ordinary thought.

Negation – the negation of a proposition is its denial.

Nihilism – a theory promoting the state of believing in nothing.

Omnipresence – the capacity of God to be present everywhere at once.

Onomastics – the branch of semantics that studies the etymology of proper names.

Ontological argument – St. Anslem – "that than which nothing greater can be conceived."

Ontology – branch of metaphysics concerned with what exists.

Open sentence – sentence containing free variables, and it is not interpretable as true or false.

Open texture – however tightly we define an expression, it remains not able to satisfy all answers.

Oppression – the unjustifiable placing of a burden.

Orthodox – Greek – right belief, a belief that is commonly shared.

Ostensive definition – to show what is intended.

Over determination – a conclusion proved in a number of independent ways.

Panglossian – to be ludicrously optimist.

Pantheism – the view that God and universe is one.

Paralogism – any fallacy or error in logic.

Paratactic – in grammar, elements of equal status are liked by punctuation, juxtaposition, etc.

Paternalism – parents right and duty to overrule children preferences in the name of their real interests, while children are not mature enough.

Perseity – a thing is acting out of its own inner nature.

Perspectivism – a view that a truth is truth from within a particular perspective.

Phenomenolism – objects are permanent possibility of sensation.

Phenomenon – manifestations in experience.

Philosophy – love of knowledge or wisdom.

Phonetics – the study of characteristics of human sounds, mainly speech.

Picture theory of meaning – a sentence that share a pictorial form.

Plenum – the concept that space is filled with matter.

Pluralism – the tolerance of different sort of things.

Posit – to put something forward as a starting point, but not necessarily known as true.

A posteriori – inductive reasoning from particular facts or effects to a general principle. A proposition is knowable *a posteriori* if it is knowable on the basis of experience.

Pragmatism – a philosophy of meaning and truth.

Procedural justice – the justice concerned with the application of laws.

Process – a pre-defined sequence of events.

Progress – a belief in later time improvements.

Projectability – a property of predicates, a degree to which past instances can be taken to be guide to the future.

Psyche – the mind, spirit, and animating principle.

Punishment – the deliberate infliction of harm, or withdrawal of some good.

Quintessence – the fifth element, found only in celestial bodies.

Quotation – an indication that the word is mentioned rather than used.

Racism – the inability or refusal to recognize the rights of some group of people.

Refute – to disapprove.

Rhetoric – the art of using language so as to persuade or influence others.

Sapir-Whorf hypothesis – 'the thesis of linguistic determinism', the language people speak determines the way they perceive the world.

Satisfice – a solution which works, but there is no reason to believe is the best solution.

Skepticism – the denial that knowledge or even rational belief is possible.

Scholasticism – a philosophy thought in church schools and theological training in medieval period.

Self-deception – a motivated miss representation of the facts of the case.

Self-refuting – some examples: 'I am not now speaking', 'I am asleep'.

Self-respect – to uphold own scrutiny.

Semantics – the study of meaning of words.

Semiotics – the study of a symbolic system, including languages.

Sensa - 'sense data'.

Sin – going beyond plain wrong doing.

A sintesi – a proposition is knowable a sintesi it is knowable from a grouping of *a priori* or *a posteriori* elements.

Italian: *Sintesi - unificazione di vari elementi.*

Specialism – refusing respect for life of animals.

Spiritualism – a contemporary usage, the spirit of the dead communicating with the living.

Supererogatory – the deeds that are not required, and go beyond the call of duty.

Symptom – an empirically detectable feature, which can lead to a further truth.

Syntax – a grammar, or the way of expression, may be put together to form sentences.

Synthesis – the process of reconciliation a theses and an antithesis, or the outcome of a procedure. (Dialectical materialism)

Tao/Dao – Chinese, The Way – a principle of cosmic order.

Tautology – true in all interpretations.

Teleology – the study of purpose of things.

Testability – the capacity of a theory to yield predictions that can be tested.

Time – an abstract concept utilized by our intellect/mind to order, and analyze events.

Transcendental – traveling to unknown, beyond empirical experience and theoretical '*a priori*' logic.

Translation – an expression in one language has same meaning in another.

Unconscious – the brain is constantly processing information of which we remain unaware.

Uniformity of nature – the past will resemble the future.

Vague objects – an indefinite where the mountain starts and the plain ends.

Vegetarians – individuals that refuse to eat meat of dead animals.

Vegan – individuals do not eat any animal products, including eggs, or milk.

Veridical – truthful, it represents things as they are.

Volition – a mental act of trying or willing makes the difference between intentional and voluntary act, and mere behavior.

Yin/yang – an opposite but complementary force at work in the universe.

Zygote – a cell formed by the union of two reproductive cells.

References

The following is a short list of the most important references that have influenced my thinking during the last years. The opinions on this text were inductively based on personal reflection when reading the named material. Additional data was gathered during the school years and from various other sources such as Internet, magazines, TV shows, etc.

Aristotle, *Ethica Nicomachea*. Translated by Richard McKeon: New York: Random House, 1941.

Aristotle, *Organon*. Translated by Richard McKeon: New York: Random House, 1941.Includes *Categoriae, De Interpretatione, Analitica Priora, Analytica Posteriora, Topica, and De Sophistics Elenchis*.

Aristotle, *Physica*. Translated by Richard McKeon: New York: Random House, 1941.

Aristotle, *De Caelo*. Translated by Richard McKeon: New York: Random House, 1941.

Aristotle, *De Generatione et Corruptione*. Translated by Richard McKeon: New York: Random House, 1941.

Aristotle, *De Anima*. Translated by Richard McKeon: New York: Random House, 1941.

Aristotle, *Methaphysica.* Translated by Richard McKeon: New York: Random House, 1941.

Aristotle, *Politica.* Translated by Richard McKeon: New York: Random House, 1941.

Aristotle, *Rhetorica.* Translated by Richard McKeon: New York: Random House, 1941.

Aristotle, *De Poetica.* Translated by Richard McKeon: New York: Random House, 1941.

Plato, *Socratic Dialogues.* Translated by W. D. Woodhead: Toronto, New York, Paris: Nelson, 1953. Includes: Euthyphro, The Apology of Socrates, Crito, Phaedo, and Gorgias.

Plato. *The Last Days of Socrates.* Translated by Hugh Tredennick: New York, London, Toronto: The Penguin Classics, 1962.

Plato, *The Republic.* Translated by Benjamin Jowett: Norwalk: The Easton Press, 1980.

Plato. *The Trial and Death of Socrates.* Translated by Benjamin Jowett: New York: The Heritage Press, 1963.

Confucius. *The Analects.* Translated by William Edward Soothill: London, New York, Toronto: Oxford University Press, 1947.

Xu Yuanxiang. *CONFUCIUS – A Philosopher for the Ages.* China Intercontinental Press. 2009.

Zhuangzi. *Basic Writings.* Translated by Burton Watson: New York : Colombia University Press, 2003.

Mo Tzu. *Basic Writings.* Translated by Burton Watson: New York, London: Colombia University Press, 1963.

Lao Tzu. *Tao Teh Ching.* Translated by Hua-Ching Ni: Published 1979.

Averroes. *Faith and Reason in Islam.* Translated by Ibrahim Y. Najjar: Oxford: Oneworld Books, 2004.

Krell, David Farrell. *Basic Writings, Martin Heidegger*: San Francisco: Harper, 1992. Includes: Being and Time, Hegel's Concept of Experience, and On the Way to Language.

Heidegger, Martin. *Discourse on Thinking.* Translated by John M. Anderson and E. Hand Freund: New York: Harper & Row Torchbooks, 1969.

Wittgenstein, Ludwig. *Tractus Logico-Philosophicus.* Translated by D. F. Pears and B. F. Guinness: London: Routledge & Kegan Paul, 1974.

Wittgenstein, Ludwig. *Philosophical Investigations*. Translated by G. E. M. Anscombe: Oxford: Basil Blackwell LTD, 1958.

Nietzsche, F.W. *Thus Spake Zarathustra*. Translated by M. M. Bozeman: New York: E. P. DUTTON & Co., 1933.

Leibniz, Gottfried Wilhelm. *Discourse on Metaphysics*. Translated by Dr. Geo. R. Montgomery. New York: The Open Court Publishing Company, 1933.

De Spinoza, Benedict. *Ethics*. Translated by James Guttmann: London: Hafner Publishing Company (1949).

Kant, Immanuel. *Critique of Pure Reason*. Translated by F. Max Muller: New York: The Macmillan Company, 1907.

Kant, Immanuel. *Prolegomena to Any Future Metaphysics*. Translated by Paul Carusand revised by James W. Ellington: Indianapolis: Hackett Publishing Company, 1977.

Rousseau, Jean-Jacques. *Political Writings*. Translated by Frederick Watkins: Toronto: Nelson Books, 1953.

Locke, John. *Two Treatises on Government*: Birmingham, Alabama, Palladium Press, 2000.

Hume, David. *A Treatise of Human Nature*: Oxford: Clarendon Press, 1978.

Jennings, William, trans. *The Wisdom of Confucius*: New York, Boston: Books, Inc., 1900.

Hegel, Georg Wilhelm Friedrich. *Science of Logic*. Translated by A. V. Miller: New York: Humanity Books, 1969.

Heidegger, Martin. *What is Called Thinking*. Translated by J. Glenn Gray: New York, Philadelphia, London, Singapore, Sydney, Tokyo, and Toronto: 1968.

Frankl, Viktor E. *Man's Search for Meaning*: New York, London, Toronto, Sydney: Pocket Books, 1984.

Kierkegaard, Soren. *Either/Or*. Translated by David F. Swenson and Lillian Marvin Swenson: New York, London, Toronto: Anchor Books, 1963.

Kierkegaard, Soren. *Wisdom of Love*. Translated by Howard and Edna Hong: New York: Harper TorchBooks, 1962.

Kierkegaard, Soren. *Purity of Heart*. Translated by Douglass V. Steere: New York: Harper TorchBooks, 1938.

Gun-Than-gKon-mChok-bsTan-Pa'i-sGron-Me. *Hundred Ways of Elegant Saying*. Sarnath, Varanasi: Central Institute of Higher Tibetan Studies, 1991.

Descartes, Rene. *Key Philosophical Writings*. Translated by Elisabeth S. Haldane and G.R.T. Ross: London: Wordsworth Classics, 1997.

Heidegger, Martin. *On the Way to Language*: San Francisco: Harper, 1959.

Hume, David. *An Enquiry Concerning Human Understanding*. Edited by Eric Steinberg: Indianapolis: Hackett Publishing Company, 1977.

Descartes, Rene. *Philosophical Writings*: London: The Franklin Library, 1982.

Freud, Sigmund. *Civilization and Its Discontents*. Translated by James Strachey: New York, London: W.W. Norton & Company, 1961.

Durant, Will, PhD., ed. *The Works of Schopenhauer*: New York: Garden City Publishing Company, 1928.

Kant, Immanuel. *Logic.* Translated by Robert S. Hartman and Wolfgang Schwartz: New York: Dover Publications, 1974.

Berkley, George. *The Dialogues Between Hylas and Philonous*: Indianapolis: Hackett Publishing Company, 1986.

Schopenhauer, Arthur. *Essays and Aphorisms*. Translated by R. J. Hollingdale: New York, London, Sidney: The Penguin Classics, 1981.

Schopenhauer, Arthur. *The Philosophy of Schopenhauer:* New York: Carlton House, 1928

Machiavelli, Niccolo. *The Prince*. Translated from Italian: New York: Dover Publications, Inc,, 1910.

Kierkegaard, Soren. *The Concept of Anxiety*. Translated by Reidar Thomte: Princeton: Princeton University Press, 1980.

Welton, Donn, ed. *The Essential Husserl, Basic Writings in Transcendental Phenomenology*: Indianapolis: Indiana University Press, 1999.

Heidegger, Martin. *The Question Concerning Technology and Other Essays*. Translated by William Lovett: New York: Harper TorchBooks, 1977.

Hobbes, Thomas, and Edwin Curley, ed. *Leviathan*: Indianapolis: Hacket Publishing Company, 1994.

Hegel, Georg Wilhelm Friedrich. *Philosophy of Right*. Translated by T. M. Knox: Oxford: Oxford University Press, 1967.

Husserl, Edmund. *Origin of Geometry.* Translated by John P. Leavey, Jr.: Lincoln and London: University of Nebraska Press, 1978.

Nietzsche, Friedrich. *Beyond Good and Evil.* Translated by R. J. Hollingdale: New York, London, Toronto: Penguin Books, 1969.

Russell, Bertrand. *The Impact of Science on Society*: New York: Simon and Schuster, 1953.

Dewey, John. *Democracy and Education*. New York: The Free Press, 1916.

Whitehead, Alfred North. *Science and Philosophy*: New York: Philosophical Library, Inc., 1948.

Derrida, Jacques. *Acts of Religion*: New York: Rutledge Publishers, 2002.

Lyotard, Jean-Francois.

The Postmodern Condition: A Report on Knowledge. Translated by Geoff Benningtion and Nrian Massumi: University of Minnesota Press, 1988.

Lyotard, Jean-Francois. *The Inhuman*. Translated by Geoffrey Bennington and Rachel Bowlby: Stanford: Stanford University Press, 1991.

Manor, Eli. *The Infinity and Beyond.* New York, London, Tokyo: Princeton University Press, 1991.

Hawking, Stephen. *A Brief History of Time*: Toronto, New York, London, Sidney, Auckland: Bantam Books, 1988.

Searle, John R. *Philosophy in a New Century*. Cambridge: Cambridge University Press,2008.

Searle, John R. *Making the Social World:* Oxford: Oxford University Press, 2010.

Chomsky, Noam, and Edward S. Herman. *Manufacturing Con$ent*: New York: Pantheon Books, 2002.

Chomsky, Noam, and Anthony Arnove. *The Essential Chomsky*: New York London: The New Press, 2008.

About the Author

Yoji K. Gondor is an American engineer and a freelance philosopher. He is originally from Transylvania; a place that has molded his original way of dealing with the abstract absurdities that life provides. He has an interest in the areas of logic, epistemology, philosophy of science and metaphysics. He is the author of a self-gathered collection of philosophical quotes that is presently in preparation for publication.

CPSIA information can be obtained at www.ICGtesting.com
Printed in the USA
LVOW12s1532041113

359953LV00016B/1026/P

9 781481 015370